Soldiers, Cavaliers, and Planters

Soldiers, Cavaliers, and Planters

Settlers of the Southeastern Colonies

Kieran Doherty

The Oliver Press, Inc.
Minneapolis

Page 2: This frontispiece for John Ogilby's America, *a collection of writings published in 1671 about the New World, shows how American Indians and unknown beasts had captured the European imagination.*

The Oliver Press, Inc.
Charlotte Square
5707 West 36th Street
Minneapolis, MN 55416-2510

For Lynne

Library of Congress Cataloging-in-Publication Data
Doherty, Kieran.
Soldiers, cavaliers, and planters : settlers of the southeastern colonies / Kieran Doherty.
p.   cm.—(Shaping America ; 2)
Includes bibliographical references and index.
   Summary: Discusses the lives of nine people who were responsible for the founding or fostering the growth of settlements in the colonial American South.
ISBN 1-881508-51-X (lib. bdg.)
1. Southern States—History—Colonial period, ca. 1600-1775—Biography—Juvenile literature. 2. Colonists—Southern States—Biography—Juvenile literature. [1. Southern States—History—Colonial period, ca. 1600-1775. 2. Colonists—Southern States.] I. Title. II. Series.
F212.D64   1999
975'.02—dc21
                                   98-10959
                                     CIP
                                     AC
ISBN 1-881508-51-X
Printed in the United States of America
05 04 03 02 01 00 99   8 7 6 5 4 3 2 1

Contents

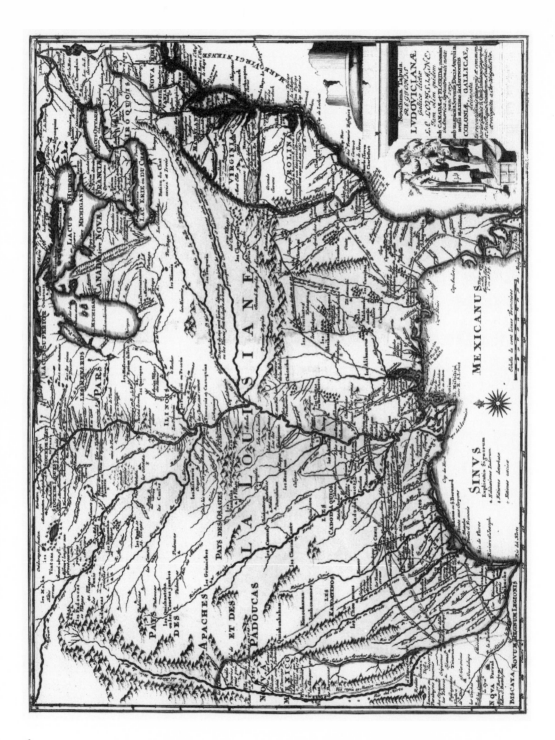

6

Introduction

⸺◆◆◆⸺

This book tells the stories of the Europeans who settled what became the southeastern United States. Their lives were full of heroism and endurance and sometimes brutality. The struggles of the English, Spanish, and French explorers and founders of the Southeast shaped the nation. But long before the Spanish heard tales of gold cities in the New World, long before the disappearance of the English settlers on Roanoke Island, and long before Pocahontas rescued Captain John Smith from death at the hands of her people, other men and women had ventured into these lands.

The first immigrants made their way to the North American continent more than 30,000 years ago. Hunters crossed the Bering Strait from Siberia to far western Alaska on what is called the Bering Land Bridge, a dry causeway that then joined North America and Asia. These earliest settlers became the peoples now known as American Indians.

Over a period of thousands of years, the descendants of these north Asian hunters spread to the south and east until they peopled the Americas

On this 1716 French map of what became the United States, most of the land is identified by the names of Indian groups who lived there. The map also shows the French territory—La Louisiane—spread over much of the country. In contrast, the English colonies from New York (Nova York) to Carolina are crowded along the East Coast. English maps, like the 1727 one on page 111, portray a much different division of territory.

from the northern reaches of Canada to the southern tip of Argentina. The groups developed diverse cultures in their different environments. Some people migrated to what is now the southwestern United States and carved out their homes in high cliffs that provided security from enemies. Others made their way to the Great Plains between the Mississippi River and the Rocky Mountains, where they grew corn and hunted buffalo. Some traveled, probably in dugout canoes, to the islands of the Caribbean. As the centuries passed, many others migrated to what is now the southeastern United States.

Along the eastern seaboard, extending north and west to the Great Lakes, were the Indians of what is known as the Algonquin Nation, named after the Algonquian language they spoke. Some major tribes of the southeastern Atlantic Coast region were also Algonquins. Most notably, the Algonquin Powhatans had created a confederacy of 200 villages ruled by Chief Powhatan. The Algonquins of the Southeast lived by hunting and foraging for food in the rich lands they inhabited. These mostly peaceful people also grew tobacco, hemp, and various food crops.

The Creeks were the most powerful Indians of the Southeast. Like most southeastern Indian tribes, the Creeks, Chickasaws, and Choctaws spoke Muskogean languages. The Cherokees of the Great Smoky Mountains and the Tuscaroras, leaders of a large confederacy in North Carolina, spoke an Iroquois dialect. South Carolina's Catawbas were a confederacy of Sioux-speaking tribes.

A confederacy was a group of tribes that joined together for military or trading purposes.

The Creeks were actually a confederacy of Muskegee Indians. The English first met them along a creek in South Carolina and called them "Indians of the Creek," which was soon shortened to "Creek."

Most of the tribes between the Mississippi Delta and the Atlantic coast, including the Creeks, Chickasaws, and Choctaws, as well as the Natchez and Florida's powerful Calusas, had somewhat similar societies. These groups may have descended from earlier peoples who migrated to the region from Central America. They lived in large settlements of hundreds of residents, surrounded by pointed log fences called palisades that defended them against attack. Both men and women worked as farmers, growing corn and vegetables that supplemented a diet of fish and wild game. Many of these tribes were warlike and raided other groups of American Indians to gain wealth and to obtain captives for slavery or for ritual sacrifice. The later Seminoles of Florida were descended from a mixture of many of these Muskogean-speaking groups who had been scattered by wars and other disasters.

The long history of many of these tribes would come to a sad end in the first century of European settlement. By the end of the seventeenth century, the Indians who lived near the Europeans or met them to trade were, by and large, wiped out by disease and by wars with the Europeans and other Indian groups. Tribes still surviving in the nineteenth century could not defend their land in the Southeast against the Americans. They were forced to move further west to Oklahoma's Indian Territory.

The European settlements in what are now the southeastern states were among the oldest in North America. The Spanish came first, founding a permanent town in Florida in the mid-sixteenth century.

Before the coming of the Europeans in the 1500s and 1600s, well over 10 million Native Americans lived in North America, spread out in small villages. Because they had no contact with people from other parts of the world, American Indians had low resistance to diseases. Smallpox and other illnesses carried by the Europeans infected the natives to devastating effect. About 90 percent of the people in coastal tribes died in the first years of European settlement.

While Christopher Columbus is called the "discoverer" of America, he was most likely not the first voyager to make his way to the shores of the New World. The Vikings almost surely landed in Newfoundland around the year A.D. 1000, and Phoenician adventurers from the Middle East probably reached the Pacific coast of America about 1,000 years before the Vikings.

Founded in 1565 by the Spanish, Saint Augustine in Florida is the oldest European settlement still in existence in North America.

Soon after that, the English attempted to establish a colony on Roanoke Island in what would become North Carolina. That attempt failed, but by 1607 the English were a permanent presence in the New World, with a settlement at Jamestown in Virginia.

The years that followed the founding of Jamestown saw the beginning of settlement all along the Atlantic Coast and the Gulf Coast, from Canada to what is now the state of Florida and west to Louisiana. The settlers who braved the Atlantic Ocean and the unknown dangers of the southeastern frontier made the journey for a variety of reasons. Some came in search of religious freedom, while others sought freedom from want. A few were fortune hunters. To all, the land that became the United States offered opportunity.

This book tells the stories of the settlement of the region that today includes the states of Maryland, Delaware, Virginia and West Virginia, North and South Carolina, Georgia, Florida, Alabama, Mississippi, and Louisiana. The founding of colonies in those states encompasses some 200 years of America's early history, from the mid-1500s to the years just before the Revolutionary War.

Here you will find stories of nine individuals who were responsible for the successful European settlement of the area. Pedro Menéndez de Avilés, a Spanish soldier and adventurer, founded Spanish Florida, an empire he dreamed would stretch all the way from Canada to central Mexico. Two Canadian-born French brothers, Pierre le Moyne d'Iberville and Jean Baptiste le Moyne de Bienville, explored and settled for France the region they called Louisiana, establishing Biloxi, Mississippi; Mobile, Alabama; and New Orleans, Louisiana.

Two English adventurers had a vision of an English America in what is now Virginia and the Carolinas. Sir Walter Raleigh, a favorite of Queen Elizabeth I, was the moving force behind what is probably the most famous failure in the history of American colonization. Captain John Smith overcame that English debacle by helping to create the Jamestown settlement in Virginia. Another, less-celebrated English explorer, Henry Woodward, got the Carolina colonies on their feet with his skills at establishing trade and diplomatic relations with the powerful local Indian nations.

The wealthy Calvert family founded Maryland as a refuge for Roman Catholics who were suffering persecution in England. General James Oglethorpe, another influential Englishman, planned Georgia as a haven of another sort. In his vision, the colony would give the poor and unemployed of England a chance to prosper.

Not all the founders of the southeastern frontier had the noble goals of Oglethorpe and the Calverts. Some hoped to find gold and other treasures. The sole interest of others was in expanding their home nations' territories in the New World. No matter how imperfect their motivations were, however, the lives of these leaders stand as vibrant examples of how courage and tenacity can triumph against the odds.

Chapter One

Pedro Menéndez de Avilés
and
Spanish Florida

On a September day in 1574, a Spanish adventurer and explorer named Pedro Menéndez de Avilés wrote a letter to his nephew Pedro Menéndez Marqués. In that letter, he complained that his work in Spain was "unbearable." His only reward, he said, was being of service to "God and . . . the King." He longed instead to be in the Spanish colony of Florida. "After the salvation of my soul," wrote the explorer, "there is nothing in this world I desire more than to see myself in Florida, to end my days saving souls."

Menéndez, then 55 years of age, had spent his entire life serving his God and his king as he thought best. He explored large parts of the New World of the Americas. He endured danger and hardship to carry the Roman Catholic faith to the American

Pedro Menéndez de Avilés (1519-1574) wrote in his will, "It is my purpose and the object of my zeal to ensure that Florida is populated forever, so that the Holy Gospel might be spread and implanted in those provinces."

Indians of Florida. At times, he waged cruel war against the enemies of Spain. Most importantly, in 1565 he established the Spanish colony of Florida and founded Saint Augustine, the oldest European city still in existence in the United States.

Pedro Menéndez de Avilés was born on February 15, 1519, in the city of Avilés, Spain. He was 1 of 20 children of Juan Sanchez de Avilés and his wife, María. Juan was a soldier who had fought gallantly for the king of Spain. María was the daughter of a high-born family.

Although commonly referred to as Pedro Menéndez, Pedro's full name adds "de Avilés." That name was given to the family by the monarch when his ancestors were granted lands around the seaport of Avilés. The family continued to bask in royal favor. While Pedro was growing up, Spain was enjoying what is known as its "Golden Age." Under the rule of King Charles I, Spain was the strongest and richest nation in the world.

After his father died and his mother remarried, Pedro was sent to live with a relative when he was about 8 years old. He soon ran away from his guardian's home and was gone for six months before he was found and brought back. Perhaps as a way to tame the wild youth, Pedro's family betrothed him (promised him in marriage) to a distant cousin, Ana María de Solís, who was herself only 10.

Because Pedro had 19 brothers and sisters, he did not inherit very much money from his father's estate to live on when he got older. The teenager decided he would seek his fortune at sea. Pedro

King Charles I also held the title Charles V, the Holy Roman Emperor. While he was supposed to be the civil ruler of all Christians—just as the Pope was their spiritual ruler—no Holy Roman Emperor actually was that powerful.

became a sailor on board a ship that was battling French pirates. These pirates and the ships they sailed were known as "corsairs." After two years, Pedro Menéndez returned to Avilés and sold part of his inheritance—probably land—to purchase a small ship of his own.

During the next 20 years, Menéndez gained fame for his courage and skill in battles against the corsairs who plagued Spanish ships in the waters north of Spain. Early in that period, probably when he was about 20 years old, he and Ana María married. The couple had three daughters—Ana, María, and Catalina—and one son, Juan, who would follow his father into service in the New World's Spanish colonies. Menéndez was away from his family most of the time, sailing the seas in the service of the king.

In 1554, when he was about 35 years of age, Pedro Menéndez was appointed captain-general of what was called the Indies Fleet. This fleet of ships was responsible for transporting riches from the Spanish colonies in the Americas back to Spain, and the new captain-general made several voyages to the West Indies in this capacity. Menéndez fulfilled his dangerous duties honorably, and he was frequently promoted. But in 1563, his life seemed to be pulled out from under him. His son, who had risen to become general of the New Spain ships, was lost at sea that year. Then Pedro Menéndez was arrested. Charged with stealing from the colonial ships— unjustly, according to his biographers—he was imprisoned for almost two years.

As captain-general, Menéndez saw to it that only qualified crew members and passengers sailed and that all of the ships were properly equipped. In addition, he was responsible for the safety of the fleet and its cargo, including treasure. It was his duty to ward off attacks by pirates or other enemy ships and to detain any pirates he captured. He also punished lawbreakers among the crew.

The Spanish word *adelantado* describes someone as being "advanced." It was used as a title for colonial rulers like Menéndez because they were advancing into new territories.

Then, in 1565, Menéndez's life took a dramatic turn again. King Philip II ordered his release and gave Menéndez the appointment that would guarantee his place in history.

Philip took this action because troubling news had come to the Spanish court. A group of French Protestants had established several small settlements in the land the Spanish called "La Florida." That these people would make such a move enraged King Philip. After all, Florida had been discovered by Spaniard Juan Ponce de León and claimed in the name of Spain and the Catholic God. How dare the French Protestants move into Spain's land?

Philip believed Menéndez, with his years of colonial experience, was the man to lead an expedition to drive the French from Florida. In exchange for paying for the expedition himself, Menéndez was made *adelantado* of Florida. This appointment gave him broad powers over the lands he conquered. The adelantado was to use any means necessary to drive out "settlers who are corsairs, or of any other nations not subject to" the rule of Spain. King Philip gave the captain-general authority to explore and colonize not only what is now Florida, but also much of the known North American continent. Menéndez eventually hoped to conquer the entire eastern coastline, from Newfoundland on the north to the islands of the Florida Keys and west into Mexico. His New Spain would expand across the Mississippi River into the Southwest, and Menéndez planned to explore the Chesapeake Bay to seek a passage through the continent to the Pacific Ocean.

Florida before Menéndez

As Spain began to establish colonies in the Caribbean after the voyages of Christopher Columbus, explorers also ventured north and west searching for riches and more lands to claim. One of these explorers was Juan Ponce de León, who, in 1513, became the first European to visit the land that became Florida. He gave Florida its name either because of the flowers he saw near the coast or because he landed during Easter week (called *Pascua florida*, or the "feast of flowers," in Spanish).

This drawing shows oversized Spaniards with swords and firearms battling Indians armed with bows and arrows along the Florida coast.

The Spanish words surrounding this portrait of Juan Ponce de León (c.1460-1521) name him adelantado and discoverer of Florida.

Ponce de León had accompanied Columbus on his second voyage to the New World. A ruthless soldier—as were many early Spanish explorers—Ponce de Léon helped to crush Indian revolts on the island of Hispaniola and was made governor of the eastern part of the island (now the Dominican Republic). In reward for his work on Hispaniola, he was given a commission to explore Puerto Rico in 1508 and then became that island's governor. There he amassed a fortune in land, gold, and slaves.

A new challenge came when Ponce de León obtained a charter to discover and settle the "island of Bimini." According to legend, he was seeking the "Fountain of Youth," a spring that had magic powers to restore youth to those who drank from it. After landing near the current site of Saint Augustine, he sailed around the south end of Florida and along part of its Gulf coast before going back to Puerto Rico. He returned to Florida in 1521 to found a colony, but he was wounded by an Indian arrow upon landing. The injured explorer returned to the Spanish colony of Havana, Cuba, where he died.

In the two decades following Ponce de León's death, several explorers—including Pánfilo de Narváez and Hernando de Soto—explored Florida's interior. No serious efforts were made to establish a colony, however, until 1559, when the Spanish explorer Tristán de Luna tried to found a colony near what is now Pensacola, Florida. That settlement was abandoned after two years.

In 1564, a Frenchman named René de Laudonnière built Fort Caroline near the

Hernando de Soto (c.1500-1542) traveled for three years from Florida to beyond the Mississippi River in search of gold, silver, and jewels. The explorer died in 1542 without finding treasure. De Soto's men sunk his body in the Mississippi River.

site of today's Jacksonville. King Philip II immediately responded by sending Pedro Menéndez de Avilés to Florida to drive the French out and to colonize the region.

On June 29, 1565, Menéndez sailed from the Spanish port of Cádiz aboard his flagship, the *San Pelayo*. In his fleet were 10 ships carrying about 1,500 people, including a few families. Many of the men who sailed with Menéndez were family friends and associates who hoped to get land grants. The king supplied hundreds of soldiers for defense, and the fleet's company also included about a dozen priests and a number of stonemasons, blacksmiths, and carpenters to help build the new settlements.

Before the adelantado sailed, he learned the French Protestants were also dispatching a fleet to Florida. These vessels, under the command of Captain Jean Ribaut, were being sent to reinforce their outpost at Fort Caroline in northern Florida.

Jean Ribaut and the Frenchmen colonizing Florida were Huguenots, a large and influential Protestant sect. They were attempting to move to Florida in the midst of turmoil between Catholics and Protestants in France. In contrast to the Spanish, the Huguenots maintained mostly peaceful relations with the Indians.

Although no one knows for sure exactly where Menéndez stepped ashore, a site on the banks of the Matanzas River has been named as his landing place. Today, a soaring steel cross marks this popular tourist attraction.

Menéndez planned to make a quick passage across the ocean to Florida to arrive before Ribaut. Those hopes were dashed, however, when his fleet was struck by a hurricane in the mid-Atlantic. All but four ships were lost, and the *San Pelayo* was badly damaged. He had no choice but to proceed to the Spanish colony of Puerto Rico for repairs.

After eight days in port, the fleet, including a fifth vessel Menéndez obtained in Puerto Rico, again set sail. On August 28, it reached Florida. For several days, Menéndez and his comrades sailed along the coast, searching for a safe harbor and keeping an eye out for the French fort. On the fourth day, the fleet finally dropped anchor in a harbor that the adelantado named San Augustin, or Saint Augustine. This was the name of the Catholic saint whose feast day was celebrated on August 28, the day Menéndez first spied Florida.

While the soldiers, sailors, and would-be colonists on the ships must have wanted to go ashore, Menéndez had other plans. He needed to find the French and drive them from the territory. On September 4, as the fleet continued its search for the French settlement, it came upon four ships anchored in the mouth of what we call the St. Johns River. Menéndez had found Ribaut's fleet. Always a man of action, the commander immediately tried to attack the French vessels, but the battle ended in a standoff.

By September 7, Menéndez's fleet was back at St. Augustine. Expecting a French attack at any moment, he sent about 300 soldiers ashore to dig a

Menéndez chose the site of St. Augustine for its good harbor because the Spanish depended on ships for supplies and transportation.

trench and erect makeshift fortifications. With the building of this crude fort, the city of St. Augustine was born. The next day, following the celebration of the Roman Catholic mass by the colony's chaplain, the adelantado took possession of Florida in the name of King Philip II.

Ribaut wasted no time in contesting that claim. While the Spanish were building their fort, he sent four warships with about 600 soldiers and sailors to attack the Spanish fleet. But as the French vessels lay outside St. Augustine's harbor, waiting for the tide to change so they could close in on the Spanish, the wind suddenly grew to a gale. The French ships were blown away from St. Augustine and scattered.

One ship was driven more than 100 miles south along the coast until it finally foundered on the beach near Cape Canaveral. Almost half the men perished at sea. Ribaut and over 300 survivors of the wrecks were stranded on the barren shores.

Menéndez knew how to seize the day. With most of Fort Caroline's soldiers apparently lost at sea, the fort was largely undefended. And the soldiers remaining at Fort Caroline would not expect a raid during this weather.

"I believe we are presented with a most remarkable opportunity to serve our God and our King," he rallied his men. For two days, Menéndez led 500 soldiers on a march through the thick forest that lay between St. Augustine and Fort Caroline.

Triangular Fort Caroline was built by the French in 1564 with the help of the Timucua Indians. The outpost was already losing its struggle to survive in the wilds when the Spanish arrived.

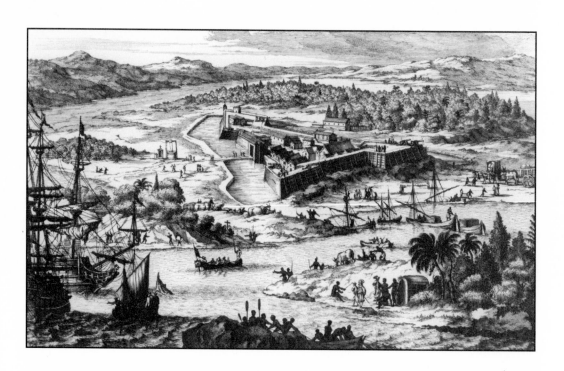

The men were drenched by driving rains and winds and often waded through water up to their hips. Late on September 19, they neared Fort Caroline and made ready to attack the fort at dawn.

The next day, Menéndez and his men struck. As they had hoped, the French were taken by surprise. About 132 were killed, and an additional 50 or 60 jumped over the fort's walls and fled into the woods. About 50 women, children, and noncombatants were spared and sent as prisoners to the Spanish colony of Santo Domingo in the Caribbean.

The victorious Spanish soldiers immediately took down the French colors and raised the flag of Spain over the fort. The adelantado renamed the settlement San Mateo in honor of Saint Matthew. Leaving a force of about 300 men, Menéndez and the rest of his men returned to St. Augustine.

Soon after their return, a native told Menéndez that a large group of white men had been seen walking on the beach toward St. Augustine. Menéndez realized that the men must be survivors of Ribaut's fleet.

Acting fast, he took about 60 soldiers to the south end of what is now Anastasia Island and found the Frenchmen. Menéndez convinced them to surrender. Now the Spanish had close to 200 exhausted and bedraggled French soldiers and sailors at their mercy, their hands bound. Questioning his prisoners, Menéndez learned that 8 were Catholic. Those 8 men were put on a small boat and taken to St. Augustine. He ordered the remaining French prisoners to be executed.

As he oversaw the massacre of the French Huguenots at Fort Caroline, Menéndez declared, "I come to hang and behead all the Lutherans [Protestants] I may find on this sea and in this land."

This grisly scene was soon repeated when over 100 more of the shipwreck survivors made their way towards St. Augustine. This time, Pedro Menéndez spared the musicians as well as the Catholics. The rest, including Ribaut, were executed. The Spanish could not have fed or sheltered their prisoners—nor could they have safely let them go—but perhaps even Menéndez's men were shocked by his mercilessness. The inlet at the south end of Anastasia Island, not far from where the French were executed, has long been known as Matanzas. That is a Spanish word that means "the slaughters."

With the last of Ribaut's men taken care of, the adelantado turned his attention to colonizing the territory and converting its native inhabitants. For the next two years, as the tiny colony at St. Augustine struggled to survive, he explored much of the vast territory from the Florida Keys to as far north as what is now the Chesapeake Bay. He also traveled inland, west toward Spain's holdings in Mexico. In addition to his explorations, Menéndez founded several small forts and missions. The Spanish built two outposts on the banks of the St. Johns River near Jacksonville, one called Santa Lucia at Cape Canaveral, and one in southeast Florida near present-day Miami. After several meetings with a powerful Calusa chief named Carlos, Menéndez constructed two forts on Florida's Gulf Coast. Spanish explorers even erected a fort on the Chesapeake Bay. Once he had established contact with the Guale Indians along the coast of Georgia, Menéndez claimed that land, which he called Guale, for Spain.

Carlos, the leader of a large band of Calusa Indians, was one of the most powerful of all the *caciques*, or Indian chiefs. Menéndez met the cacique soon after founding St. Augustine, when he sailed along the Gulf coast into what is now Esotero Bay. To create an alliance, Carlos offered his sister to Menéndez in marriage. Although he was already married, the adelantado accepted to avoid offending Carlos. Menéndez sent Carlos's sister, renamed Antonia by the Spanish, to Havana, where she was educated as a Christian.

The Spanish and the Indians

By 1565, when Pedro Menéndez de Avilés arrived in Florida, the Spanish had a long history of mistreating the Indians they met in the New World. On his first voyage for Spain in 1492, Christopher Columbus kidnapped about 25 Indians and took them back to Spain. That was only the beginning. On later expeditions, Columbus and his men tortured the Indians to force them into submission, waged war on them when they resisted, and began turning them into slaves. Many of the Arawaks and other Indians native to the Caribbean were forced to work in mines, digging for gold the Spaniards hoped would make them rich. Others were sent as slaves to Europe.

There were about 3 million Indians living on Hispaniola—now Haiti and the Dominican Republic—when Columbus first landed on the island's shores. Thanks to the slave trade, mistreatment by the Spanish, and exposure to diseases, the Indian population had diminished to about 12,000 in 1516—less than 25 years after Columbus's landing. By 1555, 10 years before Pedro Menéndez stepped ashore in Florida, there were no Indians left on Hispaniola, and the Indians of Mexico, the center of New Spain, had been conquered.

The situation in Florida wasn't much better. When the first Spaniards arrived in Florida, there were an estimated 100,000 Indians living in the area. These Indians were divided among five major tribes: the Timucuas in northeast Florida; the Ais, a small tribe living on the peninsula's east coast near Cape Canaveral; the Tequestas in the southeast; the Calusas in the southwest; the Tocobagas, who lived around what is now Tampa Bay; and the Apalachees in north-central Florida. The Guale Indians lived further north on what is now the coast of Georgia.

The relationship between the Indians and Spanish was marred from its earliest days by violence. Indians, no doubt threatened by the newcomers to their lands, often attacked Spanish ships and encampments on shore without warning. They also made a practice of sacrificing or enslaving Europeans shipwrecked on the territory's shoreline.

For their part, the Spanish began enslaving the Indians soon after Ponce de León's voyage of discovery in 1513. By the time Menéndez landed in 1565, the natives were, for the most part, filled with hatred of the Spaniards who killed them, made them slaves, raped their women, and burned their villages.

Pedro Menéndez, however, enjoyed generally good relations with the Indians he

This map shows the territory controlled by three main American Indian tribes in Florida in the period of Spanish colonization. The Timucua (Timuqua), who were French allies, held northern Florida, where both the Spanish and the French based their missions. Cacique Carlos ruled much of the Gulf Coast, and the Ais (Ays) lived in southeastern Florida.

found in Florida, at least at first. He knew he had to make the Indians his allies if the Spanish were to be successful at colonizing Florida. To his credit, Menéndez was more interested in gaining help from the Indians and converting them to Catholicism than he was in making them slaves. Because his dealings with the caciques (as the Spanish called the Indian chiefs) were friendly, he obtained the freedom of about two dozen Spanish men and women who had been shipwrecked and taken captive by various Indian groups.

Pedro Menéndez's relationship with the Guale Indians was remarkably successful. He sent missionaries to this northern section of Spanish Florida in 1566 and quickly secured ties with Guale, their chief. Chief Guale, who converted to Roman Catholicism, called the adelantado "Holy Mary's Great Chief."

It was not long, however, before the relationship between the Spanish colonists and the Florida natives soured. While Menéndez himself (and many of his officers) treated the Indians with respect, many of the soldiers did not. At the same time, Florida's Indians quickly grew to resent the Christian religion and European ways of life that were being forced on them by the Spanish settlers. Fed up once again with the European colonizers, the natives turned to violence.

Menéndez also began building Santa Elena just to the north of Guale on Parris Island. For a time, Santa Elena rivaled St. Augustine as Spanish Florida's capital city. After these expeditions, Menéndez left for the Caribbean in October 1566, leaving others to govern in his place. He established a vital supply line from Spanish Cuba to Florida, ensuring that the colonists would have the food and arms they needed to put the Florida settlements on a solid footing. While he was gone, soldiers at Santa Lucia, San Mateo, and St. Augustine mutinied, but the adelantado quickly restored order on his return.

Life in the wilds of Florida was difficult. While the waters teemed with fish and the forests with game, such food as corn and other grains was always in short supply. Indian attacks were also a danger. Even though Menéndez tried to maintain peaceful relations for trading and missionary work, his soldiers often assaulted Indian men and raped women. On May 18, 1567, the adelantado set sail for Spain, where he hoped to obtain additional money, men, and supplies to support his settlements.

The homecoming was joyous. When he and a handful of his men sailed into the harbor at Avilés, they were cheered as heroes. Menéndez was greeted there by his wife, Ana María, and their daughters. Pedro and Ana María probably looked like strangers to each other. Menéndez had been home only four times during his colonial service.

In Madrid, Menéndez gave King Philip his report of the Spanish venture in Florida. He had discovered some two dozen harbors along the coast

Now in South Carolina, the settlement of Santa Elena was once the capital of Spanish Florida. After 1568, Menéndez turned his attention to Santa Elena and built his family seat there. His wife and children moved to the new capital in 1571.

Menéndez's designs on the New World were grand. Under his direction, a party led by Juan Pardo explored west of Santa Elena, crossing the Appalachian Mountains and establishing several short-lived inland forts. Another group, under Menéndez's nephew Pedro Menéndez Marqués, surveyed the coast as far north as Newfoundland.

According to legend, after Menéndez killed the French soldiers at Fort Caroline he put a note over their bodies saying, "I do this not to Frenchmen but to Lutherans." Dominique de Gourgues, the legend continues, pinned a sign to slain Spaniards after retaking the fort. "I do this not as to Spaniards," he wrote, "but as to traitors, robbers, and murderers."

of the territory and his inland explorations were also promising. A half-dozen Indians had accompanied him to the Spanish court so the king could see the Native Americans of the Florida region. The adelantado explained how he had made treaties of friendship with almost all the chiefs he had met. After showing King Philip that his explorations were fruitful, Menéndez convinced the king that he needed more men, ships, and funds.

To repay the commander for the losses he had suffered in Florida, the king named him governor of Cuba and captain-general of the Royal Armada. He also gave Menéndez cash payments and property. King Philip had paid for about half of the first expedition's soldiers and for one ship, and he had sent another ship of supplies and more men the next year. But now he promised to send regular subsidies to help support Spanish Florida.

While Menéndez received these pledges from the king, word came from Florida that a French party led by an adventurer named Dominique de Gourgues had raided three Spanish forts. Fort San Mateo had fallen to the French. Scores of Spanish soldiers were killed in the attacks on the forts, and all those captured were executed. The French showed no more mercy than the Spanish.

Menéndez wanted to go back and defend his colony, but his new appointments were demanding. Then more bad news arrived. In the late summer of 1568, while in Havana, Cuba, protecting Spanish ships loaded with treasure against pirates, Menéndez learned the colonists in St. Augustine were desperate.

The help promised by the king had not been sent, and the people were hungry and in rags.

The colonists, who were in no state to defend themselves, were also having problems with the Florida Indians. Carlos, a once-friendly Calusa chief and powerful leader on the Gulf Coast, had rebelled at the idea of living in peace with Tocobaga Indians near Safety Harbor, Florida. The Spaniards killed Carlos, but then the Calusa Indians struck back in retaliation and the Spanish were forced to abandon their Gulf Coast and southern Florida outposts. Now four of the settlements Menéndez had founded were no longer in existence.

Saturiba, cacique of a band of Timucua Indians living near Fort San Mateo, helped the French raid the Spanish fort.

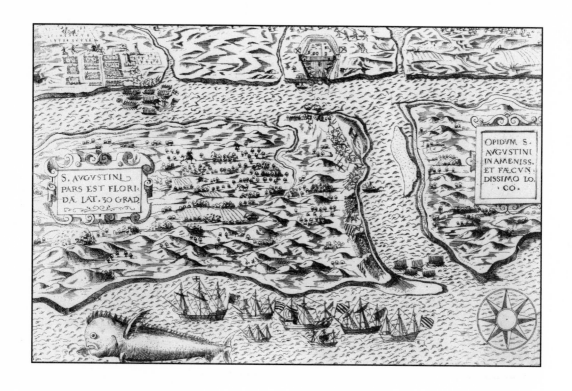

St. Augustine in 1585-1586. Sea beasts like the fanciful monster at the bottom of the map terrified sailors.

Because of his other duties in the Caribbean, it was not until late 1571, more than four years after leaving Florida, that Menéndez was once again able to visit the land he had grown to love. Since he was under orders to protect the treasure fleets in the Caribbean, the adelantado could only stay a short time. He unloaded supplies for the colonists and tried to buoy their spirits.

Menéndez would never see Florida again. In April 1572, he returned to Spain. By that time, only St. Augustine remained of his settlements in what is now Florida. Santa Elena and the Guale settlements were still flourishing, but, except for St. Augustine, the outposts south of the current Georgia border had all been wiped out by Indians who had grown tired of mistreatment by the Spanish colonizers. It now appeared to Menéndez that the only way for Florida's colonies to succeed was to wage war on the Indians who refused to accept the Catholic faith and Spanish rule. He asked the king for permission to attack the Indians and to export as slaves any Indians he captured. Mercifully, his request was denied.

Instead, in 1573, the captain-general was given orders to prepare a large fleet of warships for the king. This fleet was to wage war against the English, who were becoming a power to be reckoned with on the seas of the world. The 54-year-old accepted his new obligations and got to work. But he was not happy. On September 7, 1574, Menéndez sat down to write to his nephew. Soon, he hoped, he would "be at liberty to go at once to Florida, not to leave it as long as I live; for that is all my longing and happiness." By that time he was tired, worn out by his work, and very ill, probably from typhus. Ten days later, on September 17, 1574, Pedro Menéndez de Avilés, the founder of Florida, died.

Menéndez and his family had lost everything in their attempt to create Spanish Florida, and the founder received little from his native country in return for his sacrifice. One biographer declared that to Menéndez, Spain "owes a monument" and added that history owes the leader "a book, the muses a poem."

In 1588, 14 years after Menéndez's death, a Spanish fleet called the Spanish Armada finally attempted to crush England. The 130 ships and 30,000 men were met by a nation prepared to rule the seas. The English navy scattered the great fleet and was the world's naval superpower for the next three and a half centuries.

Florida after Menéndez

Spanish Florida continued in turmoil under Pedro Menéndez's successor, his son-in-law Hernando de Miranda. St. Augustine again became the colony's capital after an Indian war forced settlers to abandon Santa Elena in 1576. King Philip II took over the troubled colony and then appointed Pedro Menéndez Marqués, explorer and nephew of the old adelantado, as the new governor. But 10 years later, Sir Francis Drake burned St. Augustine to the ground.

Despite Drake's destruction, Spanish Florida survived for more than 150 years. Then England began chipping away at the colony. Its northern border was set at its current location after James Oglethorpe drove the remaining Spanish from his Georgia colony in 1742. Finally, the rest of Florida was turned over to England in 1763, in the wake of the Seven Years' War.

Under British rule, Florida was divided into two territories, East Florida and West

The greatest military hero of his time, Andrew Jackson (1767-1845) was first sent to Florida in 1817 to fight Seminole Indians who were raiding settlements in Georgia.

Florida. Most Floridians remained loyal to England during the Revolutionary War because the English had devoted considerable money and energy into making their colony economically successful. When the Treaty of Paris was signed in 1783, ending the war, Florida was returned to Spain.

In 1819, Spain transferred Florida to the United States after years of strife with colonists of British ancestry. Andrew Jackson, who would later become America's seventh president, was the first military governor of Florida, serving in 1821. The following year, Florida was organized as a United States territory, and William Duval was named its governor. Settlers streamed into the area, including Indians from the regions just to the north.

Even before Florida became part of the United States, there were conflicts between the Seminole Indians and the nation to the north. Tensions increased with the influx of white settlers, not least because the Seminoles sheltered escaped slaves. In fact, the Seminoles adopted so many African American refugees that they became an ethnically mixed tribe. The United States devoted tremendous resources to fighting the Seminoles in the Seminole War, and the Indians were defeated by 1842. While many of the Seminoles were removed to Oklahoma, a small band moved south and hid out in the wild swamp called the Everglades. The descendants of this band still live in southern Florida.

The Indian resistance quashed, Florida joined the nation as a slave state in 1845.

Seminole leader Coacoochee, or Wild Cat, refused any peace treaty with the United States that did not guarantee freedom for the formerly enslaved black Seminoles.

Chapter Two

Sir Walter Raleigh
and the
Lost Colony of Roanoke

The story of the English colonization of the southeastern coastal regions began—and almost ended—with the attempt to found a colony on Roanoke Island, off the coast of what is now North Carolina. Queen Elizabeth I, charmed by the New World dreams of her court favorite, Sir Walter Raleigh, made this one attempt—England's first—at a colony. Victims of a passing fancy, the Roanoke colonists would disappear with barely a trace, and England would not have a successful colony until 1607, four years after Elizabeth's death. The fate of the colonists remains one of the great mysteries of American history.

      Sir Walter Raleigh was born in about 1552 in Devon, England, to a well-respected but financially strapped family. At about age 16, Walter enrolled in

Poet, scholar, military hero, and adventurer, Sir Walter Raleigh (1552?-1618) was a great romantic figure in his time. He was even rumored (without much evidence) to be Queen Elizabeth's lover.

Oxford University. Like many young gentlemen of his time, he did not stay to complete his education. Instead, Walter left to become a soldier after about a year. For the next six years, he fought on the side of the Huguenots (French Protestants) in the religious wars then being waged in France.

The 23-year-old went to London sometime in 1575. Moving in literary circles where he was prized for his wit and conversation, Raleigh began writing verses that gained him some fame as a poet (and many of his poems are still loved today). The young writer let his imagination wander in another direction, too. He and his half brother Sir Humphrey Gilbert began planning to sail to America in search of adventure and riches.

The time was right for Raleigh, then about age 24, and Gilbert, 14 years his senior, to dream of finding wealth as colonists. Both were out-of-work soldiers. Although they were gentlemen, their extended family was so poor that Walter's birthplace had to be sold. Raleigh and Gilbert were ready to seek glory for England and themselves in the New World. Since England considered Spain an enemy, the queen encouraged seizure of Spanish ships—and their cargos of treasures from the New World.

Gilbert petitioned Queen Elizabeth for a commission to go in search of the fabled Northwest Passage through the North American continent to the Pacific Ocean. He made no secret of the fact that he and Raleigh also planned to take Spanish ships for England. Queen Elizabeth's Privy Council (a group of close advisors) approved the venture.

The Search for a Route to the Orient

The North American continent was long believed to be a narrow island. Many early European explorers sought a water route through it to the Pacific Ocean. The discovery of such a route would have enabled ships to sail to trading centers in Asia more directly and quickly. The silk, tea, and spices that Europeans desired were available only in Asia, and the shorter the trip, the greater the profits for the merchants.

European sailors thought the route was to the north through present-day Canada.

The first man to search for the Northwest Passage, as it was called, was the French navigator Jacques Cartier, who in the 1530s and 1540s thought it might be what we know today as the Saint Lawrence River. Other explorers who hoped they had found the passage were Sir Martin Frobisher, an Englishman who discovered Frobisher Bay on Canada's Baffin Island in 1576, and Henry Hudson, who thought the Hudson Bay in Canada, which he explored in 1610, might lead to the passage.

Explorations of new territory were dangerous. Henry Hudson was so determined to find the Northwest Passage that he forced his crew to stay in the Hudson Bay through the 1610-1611 winter. Starving and ill, the crew mutinied the next summer and left Hudson, his young son, and seven crew members to die in the wide Canadian waters.

They could claim for England any "remote and barbarous lands" that were "not already possessed by Christians." The two then raised money from private investors. In 1578, their fleet set sail.

From the beginning, this expedition appeared doomed to failure. Thrashed by storms just after departure, the ships had to return to port for repair. Setting out again, they were attacked by Spanish ships in a fierce battle off Cape Verde on the west coast of Africa. One of the ships was sunk in that battle, and everyone on board drowned. The other ships in the fleet turned tail and headed back to Devon. All, that is, except the *Falcon*, the ship under Walter Raleigh's command. For the next six months, Raleigh searched the Atlantic for some Spanish ship he could take as a prize. Much of his crew was killed in his one sea battle, and Raleigh finally had to return to port, his ship storm-damaged and his remaining crew near starvation.

Raleigh and Gilbert lost a small fortune on their ill-fated adventure. Probably to earn money while waiting for a chance to take to the sea again, both men signed up to fight in Ireland, where the Irish were staging one of a series of rebellions against their unwelcome English masters. Raleigh was made a captain of infantry in the Irish province of Munster.

The new infantry captain was better at killing Irish rebels than at finding Spanish treasure ships. His name was soon feared after he oversaw the massacre of some 600 men surrendering a military post. The victims were Spanish and Italian soldiers who were in Ireland to defend their fellow Catholics.

By the time Raleigh went to Ireland, England had already spent four centuries trying to colonize the country and dominate the native people. But the battles were now more brutal than before because England feared an invasion from the mostly Catholic land.

In 1581, Raleigh returned to England a hero. His triumphs in Ireland made him popular in the court of Queen Elizabeth. Raleigh dressed the part of the swaggering gentleman. Wearing his pearl earrings and velvet and silk finery, he was one of the most flamboyant men in the court at a time when men tried to outdo each other with the lavishness of their costumes. He acted just as outlandish as he dressed. According to one story, he spread a sumptuous cloak—his best one—across a mud puddle so Elizabeth could cross it without getting her feet wet.

Perhaps as a result of that gallantry, Raleigh soon became one of Queen Elizabeth's favorites. While there was some talk of a romance between the two, there is no proof they were ever lovers. It is more likely that Elizabeth, then about 50 years of age, simply enjoyed the younger man's company.

Being a favorite of the queen had its rewards. Raleigh was assigned the dashing role of the captain of the Queen's Guard. Queen Elizabeth also gave him a house in London, two estates in Oxford, land in Ireland, and the monopoly for the sale of wine licenses and the export of woolen cloth. In addition, he was knighted Sir Walter Raleigh in 1584.

During these years, Raleigh did not lose his desire to explore and colonize faraway lands. While he dressed like a dandy, he was at heart a soldier and an adventurer. But Elizabeth would not allow him to leave the court. Finally, in early 1584, following Sir Humphrey Gilbert's death on an expedition to Newfoundland, Raleigh was given his half brother's patent to colonize America in the name of the queen.

Queen Elizabeth I (1533-1603) hid her Protestant faith during the rule of her Catholic half sister, Queen Mary I. Then, during her long reign that lasted from 1558 to her death in 1603, Elizabeth faced the threat of war with Catholic Spain and France—as well as Catholic plots on her life.

Sir Humphrey Gilbert

Sir Humphrey Gilbert, Raleigh's half brother, was born in about 1538. Like Raleigh, he studied briefly at Oxford before leaving school to join the English army. An accomplished soldier, he fought in France, Holland, and Ireland, eventually reaching the rank of colonel and being knighted for his services.

When he was a young man, Gilbert became fascinated by the idea of establishing a colony in North America and finding the Northwest Passage. That interest led to his joint efforts with Raleigh.

The expedition that cost him his life left England in June 1583 and reached St. John's Bay in Newfoundland two months later. Gilbert claimed the territory in the name of Queen Elizabeth I. The English hoped to turn Newfoundland into a fishing colony, for European fishermen had been sailing there since the early 1500s to enjoy the area's bounty.

Gilbert would not be the one to establish the colony, however. His overloaded ship, the *Squirrel*, sank in the midst of a terrible storm on the return voyage to England. According to a witness watching from another vessel, Sir Humphrey Gilbert sat calmly on the deck, reading a book as his ship was sinking.

Raleigh did not plan to find a place where English people could start a new life. Instead, he hoped to use the colony as a military base to attack Spanish ships carrying treasure from the New World.

As soon as he had his patent, Raleigh financed and arranged an expedition to find a location for a military colony that was close enough to the Spanish colonies in Florida to serve as a base for privateering. In the summer of 1584, this expedition, without Raleigh, visited the coast of what is now North Carolina. The sailors found an inlet to the waters of Albemarle Sound through the island chain off the coast. After establishing contact with the native

Privateers were authorized by the English government to seize enemy ships and their cargos.

inhabitants of the area and spying Roanoke Island—safely shielded from probing Spanish eyes by the islands of the Outer Banks—the expedition returned to England.

The news the sailors brought back was good. The fertile land was filled with plants and wild game, and the climate was pleasant. In fact, the commander claimed, "The earth bringeth forth all things in abundance, . . . without toil or labor." Satisfied, Sir Walter began making plans to establish a colony there. He called the land "Virginia" in honor of Elizabeth, known as the "Virgin Queen" because she never married.

The second Raleigh expedition was made up of seven ships carrying 600 men, most of whom were soldiers and sailors hoping to make their fortunes on privateering missions. Unfortunately for Raleigh, the queen continued to demand that he stay in London. When the fleet set sail on April 9, 1585, he could only wave good-bye from the shore.

Perhaps if Raleigh had been allowed to lead his own colonists, history might have turned out differently. By all accounts, he was an excellent leader. As it was, the Virginia expedition was led by Ralph Lane, who was to be the colony's first governor, and a cousin of Raleigh named Sir Richard Grenville. Disasters plagued them from the start. The fleet ran into storms soon after sailing. Food and other supplies were wasted during long delays in the Caribbean while Grenville searched for Spanish treasure ships to plunder. Friction soon arose between Grenville and Lane.

Greedy for riches, Sir Richard Grenville (1542?-1591) would later die trying to capture Spanish treasure ships.

"Virginia" before Raleigh

Named for Queen Elizabeth I, the "Virgin Queen," the Virginia of Sir Walter's time stretched all the way from French holdings in present-day Canada to the northern borders of Spanish Florida. It referred to all of North America that might easily be claimed and settled by the English. While what is now the state of Virginia got its name from this territory and is within its boundaries, Sir Walter Raleigh's settlement in Virginia was in present-day North Carolina.

The first Europeans to visit the North Carolina coast were a group of French sailors led by Italian explorer Giovanni da Verrazano. These explorers traveled along the coastline in 1524 and probably came ashore for water and supplies. In 1526, a group of Spanish sailors and African slaves established a small colony, probably at the mouth of the Cape Fear River in North Carolina. Within a year, however, most of the Spanish were killed in an Indian attack, while the enslaved Africans escaped. If they survived, these Africans were the first non-Indian residents of America. Although an expedition led by Hernando de Soto also explored part of what is now western North Carolina in 1540, Europeans neglected the region for years. Then the English arrived.

When the English colonists first landed on the shores of the Carolinas, American Indians had been living in the region for

Like so many other explorers before and after him, Giovanni da Verrazano (c.1480-1527?) was searching for a route to Asia when he surveyed the east coast of North America.

about 10,000 years. The first Indians who met the English settlers on Roanoke Island were Carolina Algonquins, members of a widely scattered group of tribes that shared the Algonquian language. The Roanoke, Croatoan, Choanoke, and Secotan Indians were Algonquins who lived in small villages and farmed the surrounding land.

Somehow, the party managed to make it to North America, landing at Roanoke in late June. There, however, the expedition's woes continued. The waters around the island were too shallow for the larger ships, and most of their food was lost when a supply ship ran aground. Although they were now dependent on the Indians for food, Grenville, a bad-tempered man, almost immediately started trouble with the Secotans, one of several small Algonquin tribes in the region. For the alleged theft of a cup, Grenville ordered the destruction of the Secotan village and fields. When the men weren't wreaking havoc among the American Indians, they were searching for gold and pearls instead of doing the hard work of planting a colony.

But not everything about the Virginia expedition was a disaster. This time, the colony had interpreters to communicate with the Indians. Two were Indians who had been brought back to England by the first mission, and the third was scientist Thomas Hariot. Hariot also helped direct a study of the local resources and possible crops to be grown in the region.

The illustrated title page of Thomas Hariot's A Brief and True Report of the New Found Land of Virginia.
This book, with Theodore de Bry's wood-cut reproductions of John White's paintings of the New World, captured the imaginations of Europeans.

The Indians in the Albemarle Sound region lived in neatly plotted villages like this one at Secota, pictured in Hariot's book. They grew tobacco (lower left), and they planted corn (the fields at right) at different times during the year so that they would have a continual supply of food.

By late July, as the commanders tried to find a better location for the settlement, the colonists built a small fort, surrounded by a palisade for defense, and a few rough houses. More than 70 years after Spaniard Juan Ponce de León first landed in Florida, the English finally had a foothold in America.

At the end of August, Grenville set sail for England, promising to return the next spring with more colonists and much-needed supplies. He left behind 107 men, woefully short of food and other necessities. They were entirely reliant on the Indians to provide food over the winter months. Since it was a drought year, food was scarce even for the Indians. On one mission inland to search for gold, the men were forced to eat their dogs to avoid starvation. By the spring, relations with the Indians had deteriorated. While Chief Menatonon of the Choanokes still helped the English—not least because they held his son hostage—Chief Pemisapan of the Roanoke Indians had turned against the invaders in April 1586. Without enough food to support the colony, the English had to scatter and forage to survive.

Still, Grenville did not arrive, and the situation was worsening. When Governor Lane heard that Pemisapan was plotting a conspiracy to drive out the English, he acted rashly. On June 1, 1586, Lane's men assassinated the Roanoke chief. The Indians had not yet retaliated when Sir Francis Drake, the famous English sea captain, called at Roanoke one week later on his way back to England from raiding Spanish ships in the Caribbean waters. The settlers accepted Drake's offer to take them home with him.

Two Indians had returned to Europe with the 1584 Grenville expedition. One of them, a Croatoan named Manteo, served as the colonists' invaluable interpreter, guide, and negotiator. The other, Wanchese, joined Chief Pemisapan's conspiracy against the settlement.

Sir Francis Drake

Sir Francis Drake was already a celebrity when he stopped at Roanoke Island. In 1580, the admiral had become the first English person to sail around the world—a trip that lasted three years, beginning in 1577.

Born in about 1540, Francis Drake, the son of a farmer, went to sea as an apprentice to a ship captain. The young man rose quickly. He was commanding slave-trading vessels when he was still in his twenties. For a number of years, Drake attacked Spanish ships and outposts in the New World, exploits that made him famous even before his round-the-world voyage.

Drake relentlessly pursued the Spanish, putting Queen Elizabeth I in the odd position of trying to keep peace with Spain while rewarding Drake for the treasures he brought to England. The admiral gained wealth for himself on these ventures as well as the gratitude of the kingdom. Showered with gold from Drake's voyage around the globe, Elizabeth finally gave up trying to keep the Spanish king happy. Instead, she knighted her loyal subject.

The queen would not, however, allow Sir Francis Drake to invade Spain. But in 1588, when the Spanish navy launched an attack by sea on England with its great fleet, the Spanish Armada, Drake was second-in-command of the fleet that drove off the enemy and established the dominance of the English navy.

Sir Francis Drake continued his naval aggression against Spain and Portugal in the following years. As was fitting, the seafaring hero died at sea in 1596.

They were in such a hurry that they left behind three men on an inland expedition. These men were never heard from again.

Just days after Roanoke was abandoned, Sir Richard Grenville arrived with supplies. Battles in Ireland had delayed the expedition, and, as on his first Atlantic Ocean crossing in 1585, Grenville had gone hunting for Spanish ships on his way to America. After learning from the Indians that the colonists had returned to England, Grenville left a detachment of 15 men to hold the land until a new settlement could be established.

Despite the failures of the previous mission, in the spring of 1587, Sir Walter Raleigh and other investors formed a joint-stock corporation called the City of Raleigh to finance yet another colonial expedition. Unlike the earlier missions, this one was not under Raleigh's sole control. John White, an artist and veteran of the last expedition, would govern the colony with the help of a board of directors. The plan for the colony had also changed. Instead of soldiers and sailors starting a military base, the 110 colonists—including 17 women and a number of children—would establish a permanent colony in the New World. With each household receiving 500 acres, the colonists would soon be producing American goods for their home country.

Because England was preparing for a great sea battle with Spain at that time, the only ships available for the venture were the *Lion*, an old merchant ship, and two other small vessels. The City of Raleigh expedition was to stop first at Roanoke to pick up the

The settlers who returned from Roanoke with Sir Francis Drake brought with them something the Indians called *uppowoc*. Thomas Hariot wrote that the Indians cured and crushed this substance and then smoked it in clay pipes. "By sucking it . . . into their stomach and head . . . [it] openeth all the pores & passages of the body," the scientist explained. The substance was tobacco. Hariot, who became a heavy smoker, died of cancer.

A joint-stock company was an early form of a corporation. Members bought shares in the company, which would rise in value as the company gained profits. Members with a certain amount of stock could vote on company decisions.

men left behind by Grenville. Then Governor John White and the rest of the colonists were to go north to found a new settlement on the Chesapeake Bay, which, unlike Roanoke, had excellent harbors.

Nothing happened as planned. When the company landed in late July, the tiny settlement at Roanoke was empty, overgrown by the wild forest. The only signs of the 15 men left by Grenville were a few bones. Manteo, the expedition's Croatoan interpreter, found out from his people that other Indians had attacked the fort. The survivors had fled into the woods and had not been seen again. More evidence of hostility came six days after landing. George Howe, one of the governor's assistants, was murdered by the Roanoke Indians while hunting for crabs.

Despite the danger at Roanoke and the plan to continue on to the Chesapeake Bay, White remained on the island. The ship's commanders, eager to get back to privateering, had refused to take the colonists any further.

A bad situation was about to get worse. With Manteo's help, White had met with the Croatoans, who pledged to help the English negotiate for peace with the other Indians. But the Croatoans made the English promise not to demand food from them, for drought had struck hard again. Not hearing anything for several days, White decided to avenge George Howe's death. On August 8, a party of English colonists massacred a group of men, women, and children seated around a fire in the Roanoke village. In a terrible twist of fate, the victims turned

out to be Croatoans. The Roanokes had fled inland, and the Croatoans were eating the food that had been left behind. The English had lost their only allies in the brutal bungle.

But White made the best of it. He soon had the old settlement cleared of underbrush and its small fort repaired. Because they had arrived too late to plant crops and could not depend on Indian aid, more food supplies would have to be obtained from England if the colony was to survive its first winter. Reluctantly, White left with the ships in late August 1587, leaving behind his daughter, Eleanor Dare,

Nestled in shallow waters behind the islands that form the Outer Banks of North Carolina, Roanoke Island was treacherous to reach by ship. John White's map shows shipwrecks along the Outer Banks and a land dotted with Indian villages.

who was married to a colonist named Ananias Dare, and his new baby granddaughter, Virginia. Before he set sail, White told the colonists that if they moved before his return, they should inscribe the name of their destination on a tree or post, with a cross above the name if they were in danger.

In England, the government paid no attention to White's desperate pleas for aid. In November 1587, immediately upon White's return, Raleigh did outfit a small supply ship, but it did not sail, probably due to winter weather. Then the Spanish Armada made poor, abandoned Roanoke fade into the background. The Spanish were about to invade England. Because all the nation's resources were needed for defense, Queen Elizabeth would not allow ships to be used for any other purpose. When the tireless White finally won permission to take two small ships to Roanoke in April 1588, the commanders began privateering as soon as they left shore. The vessels never even got close to Roanoke.

Despite these setbacks and Raleigh's loss of interest in the expensive project, White would not give up. With Raleigh's authorization, White and other investors formed a new corporation in March 1589 to trade in the New World. Finally, in August 1590, two years after the defeat of the Spanish Armada and three years after he had left the colony, White returned to Roanoke as a passenger on a merchant vessel. Landing at the place where he had left the colonists, the former governor found no signs of life. But on a tree trunk he discovered the letters "CRO" and, carved into one of the settlement's

doorposts, the word "Croatoan." There were no crosses above either. Apparently, the more than 100 colonists had moved to Croatoan willingly.

A fierce storm forced White and the others in his party to give up any plans they had for sailing about 50 miles south to Croatoan in search of the colonists. Instead, they decided to sail to the West Indies for supplies and return the next spring, a plan that satisfied White because he believed the settlers were safe. But, like so many plans, this one also fell through. White never went to Croatoan, and no further sign of the settlement, now known as the "Lost Colony," has ever been found.

The houses at Roanoke had been destroyed, and the only personal belongings at the site were John White's. It was distressing for him to find his armor rusted through, his books torn apart, and his picture frames rotted from moisture.

When colonists came to Jamestown 20 years after the disappearance of the Roanoke settlement, they heard intriguing stories about their predecessors to the south. Some Indians told them that there were whites living with Indians further to the south. Another heartbreaking tale was that the Roanoke colonists had come to Chesapeake Bay near Jamestown and had lived there for 20 years. Just before the English arrived again, so the story went, the surviving settlers were massacred by the powerful Chief Powhatan.

Sir Walter Raleigh, who had spent a fortune financing the settlement of America, became entranced by more lucrative projects. His Irish plantations closer at hand were especially promising. Ironically, Roanoke governor John White would later be a colonist on one of Raleigh's holdings in Ireland. Raleigh also invested heavily in privateering in the 1590s.

But Sir Walter's adventures were far from over. In 1592 he fell from Queen Elizabeth's favor after he married Elizabeth Throckmorton, one of her ladies in waiting. The queen was so angry that Raleigh and Throckmorton had fallen in love that she had them both thrown in jail. While Queen Elizabeth soon relented and released the couple, they were banished from her court. For several years, Raleigh and his wife lived in the countryside, where he busied himself writing poetry and studying advances in science.

In 1595, Raleigh was finally able to go to the New World himself. Inspired by tales of gold in South America, the old adventurer convinced Queen Elizabeth to let him explore Guiana (now Guyana, a country on the northern coast of South America). Although that expedition failed, Raleigh, as in his younger days, had more success in the military. He served the queen as a naval officer, and an attack on the Spanish city of Cádiz in 1596 restored him to her favor. Probably as a reward, Queen Elizabeth named him governor of the Isle of Jersey in the English Channel.

After Queen Elizabeth died in 1603, Raleigh's fortunes took an immediate turn for the worse.

Enemies he had made during his long service to the queen convinced her successor, King James I, that Raleigh had conspired against him before he became king. Sir Walter's dramatic devotion to Queen Elizabeth now backfired against him, for he had refused to pledge support for James's right to the throne before her death. He was stripped of all his offices, found guilty of treason, and locked up in the Tower of London. He stayed in prison, pursuing scientific knowledge, composing poems, and beginning his most famous work, *The History of the World*.

In 1616, Raleigh convinced King James to let him lead another expedition to Guiana in search of gold. Unbeknownst to him, the English king had promised the king of Spain that Raleigh would die if he killed any Spaniards while in South America. Such battles were nearly inevitable, and Raleigh did kill Spanish colonists during his Guiana mission. The explorer returned to England to his doom. On October 29, 1618, Sir Walter Raleigh was executed under the original sentence of death handed down on charges of treason two years before.

Raleigh died an English hero. Hailed for promoting the English empire at its dawn, his book, *The History of the World*, was a bestseller. Raleigh was more popular with the English people than their king, and the explorer's fans included even the wife and son of King James I.

James I (1566-1625) was the son of Mary Queen of Scots, who had been executed for plotting against Queen Elizabeth. During James's reign, the King James Bible was translated and Jamestown, Virginia, was settled.

Ill from a tropical fever on the day of his execution, Raleigh asked to see the executioner's axe. "This is a sharp medicine," he commented, "but it is a sure cure for all diseases."

Chapter Three

Captain John Smith
and
Jamestown, Virginia

O n a December day in 1607, a 27-year-old English adventurer was captured by a group of Indian warriors near the tiny settlement of Jamestown in Virginia. After several weeks in captivity, the man, whose name was John Smith, was led into a large hut made of straw mats stretched over a wooden framework. At one end of the structure sat a scowling Indian chief named Powhatan.

The leader of an alliance of tribes that included the Powhatans, the Pamunkeys, the Potomacs, and the Chickahominies, Powhatan was one of the most powerful Native American leaders of his time. But despite his strength, he feared the Europeans who had recently come to his lands. After questioning Smith, the chief gave a signal to his men. Quickly, Indian warriors seized Smith and held him with his

John Smith (1580-1631) praised America as a place where "every man may be master and owner of his own labor and land."

head on a large stone. Others stood nearby, armed with clubs, ready to beat John Smith's brains out. Suddenly, Pocahontas, the chief's daughter, threw herself on top of Smith and held his head in her arms to protect him.

The story of Captain John Smith's rescue by Pocahontas is one of the most famous tales in American history. Yet it was just one episode in a life that reads like the script for an action-adventure movie. For John Smith spent a half century as an adventurer, soldier, explorer, and pioneering colonist. In those years, he earned lasting glory as the father of Jamestown, the first permanent English settlement in America.

Pocahontas's rescue of Captain John Smith has inspired numerous paintings, stories, and a Walt Disney movie. This dramatic painting was made in 1943.

In January 1580, John Smith was born near the village of Willoughby in Lincolnshire, a region northeast of London. He was the first child of George Smith and his wife, Alice. George Smith was a tenant farmer who worked land owned by a nobleman. The Smiths later had at least two other surviving children, a second son, Francis, and a daughter named Alice after her mother.

We know little of John's early years on the family's farm. At some point, he attended school in nearby Alford and later a boarding school further away in Louth. He left school when he was 15.

For about a year after he finished his formal schooling, John served as an apprentice in the shop of Thomas Sendall, a well-known merchant in the port town of Lynn, about 65 miles from Willoughby. A voracious reader of tales about knights, soldiers, and explorers, John hoped to go to sea and have his own adventures. The sailors at Lynn's harbor further fed the boy's fantasies.

Then, in 1596, John's father died. His mother quickly remarried, taking as her husband a farmer named Martin Johnson. While it was not unusual in the late sixteenth century for widows to marry again, John must have viewed his mother's action as a betrayal. He apparently saw her only once after her second marriage.

Not long after his father's death, John left the job with Sendall, using his inheritance to buy his freedom from the apprenticeship contract. Realizing that he was not meant to be a merchant, young John Smith had embarked on his life of adventuring.

School when John Smith was a boy began at daybreak and lasted until five in the evening, with lessons in reading, writing, religion, and Latin. John probably suffered through these long hours since he later said that even at an early age, his mind was "set upon brave adventures."

An apprenticeship was a training period during which a teenager learned a trade by working for a craftsperson. In exchange for their training, apprentices usually worked for no pay for a specified length of time.

During the next decade young Smith experienced more excitement than most people do in a lifetime. First, he spent about three years as a soldier in an English regiment in the Netherlands, where the Protestant Dutch and English were at war with the armies of Catholic Spain.

Following that adventure, 19-year-old Smith returned to England. Out of money, he was soon hired to serve as a traveling companion for a teenage nobleman—the son of the lord who owned the Smiths' land—who was touring the European continent. Smith left the young nobleman in France and traveled on his own to Scotland before returning to Lincolnshire.

Smith was always one to go to extremes, and now he spent several months living like a hermit in the woods near his hometown. He finally returned to the world a few months later to accept an attractive offer. Smith was invited into the household of a local nobleman, the earl of Lincoln, to train in horsemanship and the art of mounted warfare with an expert horseman, an Italian named Theadora Polaloga.

By 1600, John Smith was ready once again to go to war as a cavalier, a mounted soldier. Leaving his homeland for the third time, he made his way to Hungary, then torn apart by Protestants fighting Catholics and Christians fighting Turkish Muslims for territory. In Hungary, he joined a Protestant regiment, where he quickly gained a reputation as a brave and intelligent cavalier. Eventually, he was made captain of a company of 250 men.

"Being glutted with too much company," Smith remembered about himself later, "he retired himself into a little woody pasture, a good way from any town." There, by a brook, "he built a pavilion of boughs, where only in his clothes he lay."

In his autobiography, Smith claimed that he slew three Muslim warriors in three separate single-handed battles. In those days, it was not unusual for opposing armies to declare a temporary truce while two armed warriors dueled. According to Smith, he answered a challenge issued by a Turkish warrior named Turbashaw, chopping off the Turk's head while the two armies watched. He next fought a friend of the slain Muslim, killing him as well. Finally, Smith issued a challenge of his own. The Turk who answered it met the same fate as his two comrades.

In this depiction, John Smith (under the cross at right) kills his second Turkish opponent (under the Muslim crescent, a symbol of Islam).

While some historians doubt the truth of this story, the prince of Transylvania did in fact grant

The coat of arms presented to Smith by the prince of Transylvania. Transylvania is now a section of western Romania but was part of the province of Hungary in Smith's time.

The Virginia Company would later evolve into the Virginia Company of London and the Virginia Company of Plymouth (often called the London Company and the Plymouth Company). Both companies disbanded in 1609 but were later reorganized.

Smith a coat of arms, which was decorated with the heads of three Turks. Smith may have been a braggart, noted one biographer, but that does not mean his boasts were falsehoods.

In November 1602, five months after winning his duels, Smith was captured by the Turks and sold into slavery. He endured about a year of brutal treatment, but then Smith turned on his master and beat him to death. Stealing the dead man's clothes as a disguise, Smith made his way about 1,000 miles from northeastern Turkey across southwestern Russia, the Ukraine, and Poland to Transylvania. When he found his former comrades, Smith recalled, he was "glutted with content, and near drowned with joy." His commander rewarded him with a substantial amount of cash for his heroism. The world-weary cavalier eventually made his way back to England in 1604.

For a time, Smith was content to enjoy a relatively quiet life in London. Soon, however, he was swept up in the fever to explore and colonize the New World. He invested in the Virginia Company. This company was chartered in April 1606 by King James I to settle Virginia, the huge territory that stretched from modern Georgia all the way up to Newfoundland. The Virginia Company was a joint-stock company, whose members invested funds in the hope of gaining profits through trade or the discovery of gold. A few of its members, including Smith, also planned to become colonists themselves.

Three ships—the *Susan Constant*, the *Godspeed*, and the *Discovery*—were prepared for the voyage.

The three ships in the fleet sent to colonize Virginia were smaller than many private sailboats are today. At left is a replica of the 116-foot Susan Constant, *the largest of the three. Below a replica of the 68-foot* Godspeed *sails. The* Discovery *was even smaller.*

The tiny vessels were packed with supplies and out-fitted for more than 100 men. Many of these settlers were officially "gentlemen." While the gentlemen may have been brave and skilled with weapons, they were not used to working, and they were conscious of their high status. They thought they were superior to those who did menial work or those who, like Smith, were not born gentlemen.

The small fleet left just before Christmas, when an Atlantic crossing could be deadly because of winter gales. For six weeks, the vessels were trapped by bad weather within sight of England. As the ships

tossed at anchor, the settlers consumed food that was intended for use in America. In February, the fleet was finally able to leave the English Channel and begin its crossing.

When the Virginia adventurers set sail, Smith was a fairly unimportant member of the company. Perhaps he got into trouble early in their voyage because of his drive to lead. Maybe he did not show proper respect to Edward Wingfield, John Ratcliffe, or Gabriel Archer, gentleman colonists with whom he would later have many conflicts in Virginia. While we don't know for sure what Smith did, we do know that he was charged with mutiny and placed in chains. When the ships dropped anchor off the Caribbean island of Nevis, a gallows was set up to hang Smith. For some reason lost to history, the prisoner was spared. John Smith later wrote in jest that he "could not be persuaded" to use the gallows.

After leaving the West Indies, the fleet sailed north. On April 26, it sailed into Chesapeake Bay, the expedition's destination. That night, Captain Christopher Newport opened a sealed box he'd been given by officials of the Virginia Company before the colonists left England. That box held a list of names of the seven men who were to form a council to run the colony. To everyone's surprise, one of the names on the list was John Smith. But that didn't change the gentlemen's opinion of Smith. The other men on the council, including Wingfield, Ratcliffe, and Archer, simply refused to allow him to serve.

By mid-May, the colonists had chosen to settle on a point jutting into a river that emptied into the

---

In the West Indies, Smith wrote, the settlers found a natural spring "so hot, as in it we boiled pork as well as over the fire." On another island, they were reportedly able to catch hundreds of birds with their bare hands.

Chesapeake. After the colonists and their remaining supplies were ferried ashore, tents were erected for shelter and labor began on the construction of a crude fort. In honor of the king, the settlement was given the name Jamestown and the river was called the James. The site could be reached by ship but was still safe from attack by sea. Despite these attributes, Jamestown's low-lying, swampy location was to prove disastrous.

While Smith was kept off the council, he found other ways to lead. He began exploring the region

The peninsula on which Jamestown was founded is now an island.

The English did little more than put up tents before venturing off to seek gold. But after an Indian attack, they began to build a fort surrounded by a fence of pointed logs called a palisade.

around the settlement. Soon he established contact with local American Indian tribes and began trading with them for food. In June, he was finally admitted to the council because, as Smith wrote of himself, "so well he demeaned himself in this business [of working for the colony] as all the company did see his innocence." Now that he was on the council, Smith oversaw the strengthening of the crude fort that protected the colonists. With his military background, Smith alone among the colonists had the expertise to design and direct the building of the large triangular fort at Jamestown.

At first, settlers erected houses inside the triangular fort planned by Smith. Within a decade, so many houses were outside the original fort that a rectangular fenced area was added to the compound.

The Indians of Virginia

When the first European settlers arrived in Virginia, the region was inhabited by American Indians belonging to three larger groups. The hilly Piedmont region west of the coast was occupied by members of the Sioux-speaking tribes, while the Iroquoian-speaking Cherokees lived further west in the mountainous area. The Iroquoian Nottoways resided to the south, and the Susquehannas dominated the region north of the Chesapeake along the Susquehanna River. The Powhatan Indians, who were an Algonquian-speaking tribe, were spread in almost 200 villages along the coast in the region settled by the English.

Powhatan, chief of the Powhatans, had taken his name from a tribal village. He had gained his power by conquering and forging alliances with about 30 other Algonquin tribes in the region, including the Pamunkeys, the Chickahominies, and the Potomacs.

Later in June, Captain Newport departed from Jamestown on the *Susan Constant*, leaving Edward Wingfield in command as president. It would have been hard to choose a worse leader. Wingfield was disliked by many of the colonists, including Smith. In the hot and muggy summer weather of Virginia, the settlers were becoming frustrated. There was no clean drinking water, and the food supply would only last three or four more months. Then, disease swept through the colony. What the colonists called the "summer sickness" was probably malaria transmitted by mosquitoes or typhoid from the drinking water. One after another, the settlers fell sick and died. As the colony's food ran low, starvation and malnutrition also claimed lives. By the end of the summer, half the colonists were dead.

"There were never Englishmen left in a foreign country in such misery as we were in this new discovered Virginia," remembered George Percy, one of the first colonists. "Our drink was water; our lodgings, castles in the air."

Indian Wheat

An Indian Lay

The Jamestown colony was settled in a period of extended drought on the East Coast, which made an already short supply of food worse. One colonist wrote of corn (called wheat in this picture), "had it been gold with more ease we might have got it."

Accusations flew among the desperate surviving colonists. On September 10, Edward Wingfield was removed from office and arrested for allegedly hoarding food and slandering John Smith. Since Jamestown had no jail, the former president was imprisoned in the tiny boat left behind by Newport.

Smith was the savior of Jamestown that summer. His trading missions to nearby Indian villages for corn kept more settlers from dying of hunger. Organizing the remaining colonists, Smith ordered them to begin building houses. Even the gentlemen of the party had to do their fair share of work. Smith recalled that he encouraged the tired men "by his own example . . . himself always bearing the greatest task for his own share." Soon, clapboard houses with roofs of thatch or bark protected the settlers from harsh weather.

The building underway, Smith set out to explore the area further. In December 1607, he was captured by Powhatan Indians while mapping the nearby Chickahominy River. According to his autobiography, Smith and a small party were ambushed by warriors from a tribe led by Powhatan's brother, Opechancanough. Smith killed two Indians and wounded a third mortally before he was surrounded and forced to surrender. Held captive for several weeks, he was paraded by the Powhatans from village to village and was taken repeatedly before their great chief, Powhatan, who questioned him about the English colonists' plans for the territory. Finally, Powhatan reached his judgment. He sentenced Captain John Smith to die.

Powhatan as Smith depicted him on his map of Virginia. Smith recalled that although he was "taken prisoner by the power of Powhatan their chief King I received from this great savage great courtesy." This "courtesy" included a piece of land along the York River north of Jamestown.

Some people doubt the romantic story about Pocahontas saving Smith. But in many Indian tribes, captives were adopted instead of being killed, often replacing fallen warriors. This theory is bolstered by the fact that Powhatan gave Smith the Indian name Nantaquoud and granted him land. Despite the legends, there is also no evidence that John Smith and Pocahontas were in love. Pocahontas was only a child of about 13 when she met Smith. His writings show that he thought of her as a favorite niece.

Pocahontas

Pocahontas was born around 1595, and her real name was Matoaka. She was called Pocahontas because she was so playful. The teenage girl not only "hazarded the beating out of her own brains to save mine," recalled John Smith, she also convinced her father to accept him as a member of their tribe. She continued to be a great ally to the English, often visiting Jamestown.

In 1613, a few years after Captain Smith's return to England, Pocahontas was taken hostage by the English to guarantee peace with Chief Powhatan. As a captive, the young woman was taught about Christianity by Rev. Alexander Whitaker, and she converted to that religion. She also attracted the attention of John Rolfe, a tobacco planter. Her marriage to Rolfe in 1614 cemented peace with the Powhatan Indians.

Pocahontas gave birth to a son, Thomas, in 1615. The next year, Rebecca Rolfe—her English married name—traveled to England. Charming London high society, she was invited to meet the king and the royal family. The former Pocahontas was also reunited briefly with John Smith. In 1617, as Rebecca Rolfe prepared to return to Virginia, she fell ill and died, probably from smallpox. She was buried in England.

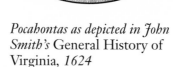

Pocahontas as depicted in John Smith's General History of Virginia, *1624*

While marriages between American Indians and Europeans were not uncommon in the colonial period, the wedding of Pocahontas and John Rolfe (above) came to symbolize a peaceful union of cultures. A celebrity in England, Pocahontas was invited to the court of King James I (below).

Smith returned to Jamestown after his rescue, no doubt expecting to be welcomed by his compatriots. Instead, he was promptly arrested. Two of his men had been killed by the Indians before his capture, and yet he had been released unharmed. The English suspected treachery. After a speedy trial, he was ordered to be hanged by his English comrades for the second time. But it was still not time for Smith to die. Shortly before the sentence was to be carried out, Captain Newport sailed into the bay with supplies for the colony and more settlers. On Newport's orders, Smith was released and restored to his place on the council.

Newport and Smith promptly returned to Powhatan's village to negotiate trading relations, and Smith continued to explore the region. In the summer of 1608, Smith led a group around the huge Chesapeake Bay and the rivers that emptied into it, looking for a likely passageway to the Pacific Ocean. This trip led to Smith's map of the Chesapeake Bay region—an extraordinarily accurate map for its time.

Meanwhile, the settlers were once again devastated by the "summer sickness." This time, of 95 colonists alive at the end of spring, about 45 perished. Perhaps this suffering reminded the survivors of Smith's leadership qualities, for they elected him president of Jamestown in September.

Upon taking office, Smith stopped exploring and settled down to run the colony's everyday affairs. Resisting the Virginia Company's demands that colonists direct all their energy into finding gold and a water passage through the continent, the new president instead enlarged the fort, making it a huge, five-sided bastion. He organized the settlers into a militia to defend against Indian attacks. Knowing that famine was a threat as winter approached, Smith also sent out trading and fishing expeditions.

In October, Captain Newport again arrived in Jamestown with more settlers. But he unfortunately did not bring adequate supplies to feed the increased population during the winter of 1608-1609. It was also a drought year, and the Indians were short of food and tired of English demands on their supplies. When Powhatan and Opechancanough resisted, Smith threatened war and forced the Indians to trade. Settlers also ate fish, shellfish, and flour made from ground-up roots.

That spring, the English finally began planting corn under the guidance of Indian prisoners. They also dug a well for safe drinking water, built houses and fish traps, and finally began to produce some naval supplies, such as tar and pitch, for the Virginia Company. Still, morale was low, and many of the colonists wanted to return to England.

Despite Smith's almost single-handed heroism in saving the colony, his enemies had convinced the Virginia Company that he was incompetent and corrupt. In the summer of 1609, Captain Samuel Argall came to Jamestown with the news that the company had ordered the leadership of Jamestown to be turned over to Lord De la Warr, who would be arriving later. Since the new charter and official orders were on another ship, Smith had to continue to govern until his replacement reached Virginia. In

By the spring of 1609, Smith may have been secretly gratified that he was the only remaining member of the original council. All the others had either returned to England or perished.

Thomas West, Lord De la Warr (1577-1618), spent little time in Virginia, but he wrote a pamphlet pleading for support for the colony. He was immortalized for his colonial work when Delaware was named in his honor in 1610.

August, four supply ships arrived, along with several of Smith's early enemies on the council.

The next month, before De la Warr came to relieve him of his duties, Smith suffered a serious injury that probably would have ended his colonial career in any case. While journeying up the James River to check on an outpost, Smith fell asleep one afternoon in his boat. Somehow, his bag of gunpowder caught on fire and exploded. Waking up with his clothes on fire, Smith leaped overboard. Although he survived, he was horribly burned. His time of effective service to the colony was over, and he departed for England in October. As far as we know, Smith never returned to Virginia.

To add insult to injury, the allegations of other former council members led to charges of treachery and insubordination against Smith. The Virginia Company, however, folded that same year and never ruled on the charges. Perhaps company leaders just needed a scapegoat as stockholders sought to reorganize and find new investors.

Down but not out, Smith told his side of the story in *True Relation* (1608) and in *A Map of Virginia* (1612). These books also praised Virginia, claiming "no place is more convenient for pleasure, profit, and man's sustenance." The adventurer still held out hope for the English colonization of America.

A few years later, Smith's prayers seemed to be answered. In 1614, the captain was hired by a group of London merchants to explore and map the coastline north of the Virginia settlement. Captain Smith was enthusiastic about what he found in the region

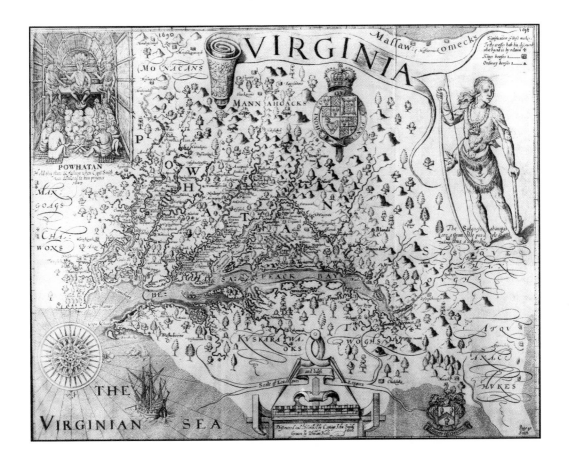

he named "New England," and he made agreements to trade fish and fur with the Indians.

The next year, Smith set out on a voyage to organize a fishing colony in Maine. Instead, he had yet another fantastic adventure. He was captured by French pirates and spent several months in captivity at sea before escaping off the coast of France. During his time with the pirates, Smith wrote *A Description of New England*, which was published in 1616. He and Prince Charles (later King Charles I) named many of New England's geographic features in that book. His maps led first the Pilgrims and then the Puritans to their promised lands.

John Smith's map of Virginia shows Powhatan in control of vast territory on the Chesapeake Bay. The Susquehanna Indians to the north, according to the note by the figure at right, "are a giant-like people and are thus attired."

Virginia after John Smith

Conditions grew so bad at Jamestown in 1610 that colonists decided to abandon their settlement. Only 60 of the 500 people at the colony when Smith left were still alive. Just as they were about to set sail in June 1610, Lord De la Warr arrived with additional settlers and supplies.

More disasters followed. Lord De la Warr and the governors who followed him were brutal to the Indians, and they would suffer for this violence. Powhatan's brother and successor, Opechancanough, led an attack that killed about one-third of the settlement's residents in 1622. Two years later, King James I revoked the Virginia Company's charter and took control of the colony.

The colony prospered economically. The tobacco John Rolfe had cultivated in 1612 soon became a lucrative cash crop. To encourage its production, the Virginia Company offered land grants to people who could fund settlers' travel to Virginia. The colony formed its own government in 1619. The house of burgesses was the first representative assembly in North America. The same year the settlers won this freedom, they imported the first black servants to Virginia, and slavery was established within the next few decades. By 1635, the

Tobacco was a New World plant long used by the Indians throughout the Americas. It was so important to the colony's economy that it became a form of money used for buying all kinds of goods.

In 1641, Massachusetts was the first colony to put slavery in its legal code. Virginia, however, had begun importing Africans as servants more than 20 years earlier. These men and women were not slaves, but they were treated more harshly than white servants and their status deteriorated to slavery by the mid-1640s. By the end of the 1600s, the success of crops such as tobacco depended increasingly on black labor.

population in Jamestown and other settlements nearby had reached 5,000.

Jamestown remained the colony's capital until 1699. The city burned in 1676 in Bacon's Rebellion, a revolt by colonists against English rule, and was never completely rebuilt before Williamsburg became the colony's new capital.

English settlement continued west from the coast toward the Blue Ridge Mountains through the early 1700s. This expansion led to conflicts between the British and the French, who had Indian allies there. The western settlement later led to disputes between Virginians and England as well. Virginia finally achieved control of its inland territory when the American colonies won their freedom from England in the American Revolution. Virginia was the tenth state to join the new United States.

Throughout its history, Virginia has provided the United States with some of its greatest leaders. Known as the "Mother of Presidents," it was the birthplace of eight U.S. presidents: George Washington, Thomas Jefferson, James Madison, James Monroe, William Henry Harrison, John Tyler, Zachary Taylor, and Woodrow Wilson.

John Winthrop (1588-1649) was the long-time governor of the Massachusetts Bay Colony. Bay Colony leaders met with Smith and read his works. They set the boundaries of their territory using his maps, and, based on his experience, they decided to take measures to govern themselves.

Smith himself never founded a colony in New England. Although the Plymouth Company gave him the title "Admiral of New England," it refused to provide finances for a colony. The Pilgrims consulted him in 1619 about their efforts to establish Plymouth Plantation, but they did not hire him to help build it. "I am near ridden to death in a ring of despair," he wrote about his failures to find funding to start his own settlement.

Captain Smith never gave up trying. He wrote *The General History of Virginia* in 1624 and *The True Travels, Adventures, and Observations of Captain John Smith* in 1630 to drum up interest among investors. Several times without success he sought commissions from the Virginia Company to return to the struggling Jamestown settlement, and he gave advice to the Puritans traveling to the New World to found the Massachusetts Bay Colony. Smith's passion for the colonization of North America was unflagging.

In his life, John Smith found all the adventure he had dreamed of as a boy. He explored territories and fought battles, winning a coat of arms and the title of "Captain." Despite his common birth, Smith rose to become president of Virginia and admiral of New England. He did not, however, gain personal wealth. By the end of his life, Captain John Smith was living alone in shabby quarters in London. The heroic soldier and explorer died on June 21, 1631. Of the English settlements in North America, he once wrote, "I may call them my children, for they have been my wife, my hawks, my hounds, my cards, my dice, and in total my best content."

The Making of West Virginia

West Virginia, which stretches west from the Allegheny Mountains to the Ohio River, was originally part of Virginia. Explorers and fur traders entered the region in the 1670s, but it was not settled for more than 50 years. German and Scotch-Irish immigrants began to move south from Pennsylvania after 1730, and more settlers made their way into the area when the British granted the Ohio Company tracts of land in 1749 to prevent French claims to the territory.

The French and their Indian allies resisted the new settlers, and the conflict heated up in the French and Indian War (1754-1763). Some colonists fled Indian massacres; others committed their own atrocities. Violence continued in the region through the Revolutionary War.

Problems with the Indians settled down after the war when an American army occupied western Virginia. The British and the French were no longer stirring up violence with the Indians, so peace probably would have come in any case.

Within a few decades, farmers in western Virginia were economically successful. Because it fed into the Mississippi River, the Ohio River became important for trade and commerce after the United States purchased the Louisiana Territory from the French in 1803. By the 1850s, the region's fine natural resources made it a center of the coal industry. Steel manufacturing also became a significant part of the economy.

Even though Virginia was a slave state, there was almost no slavery among the small farmers and merchants of the region west of the mountains. The citizens of the area resented the wealthy plantation owners further east because they dominated the state government and didn't pay attention to the concerns of those in the west.

When Virginia seceded from the United States in April 1861, the time was ripe for change. People in the western region formed their own "restored government" of Virginia in the midst of battles with the Confederate army. They decided to create their own state in October 1861. Once Union forces were entrenched, West Virginians wrote their new constitution and ratified it in April 1862. The next year, President Abraham Lincoln welcomed West Virginia into the Union as the 35th state.

Chapter Four

The Calverts
and the
Founding of Maryland

O ne day in early March 1634, two ships dropped anchor near the spot where the Potomac River empties into the Chesapeake Bay. On board the *Ark* and the *Dove* were some 220 English colonists. These men and women had come to the shores of America in search of opportunity and religious freedom.

This band of settlers had been sent to America by 29-year-old Cecil Calvert, Lord Baltimore, to found a colony. Cecil's brother, Leonard, who was one year younger, led the expedition.

These two brothers did not set out to become the founders of Maryland. Their father, George, the first Lord Baltimore, had intended to lead the colonial effort. But George Calvert died before his charter to the territory was approved.

By the time the ships reached what was to become Maryland, Virginia's Jamestown colony was on firm footing, with about 5,000 settlers.

This portrait of Cecil Calvert (touching the scroll at right) honors him as the first founder to establish religious liberty in the New World. William Penn, who followed his example, stands next to him in the wide-brimmed hat.

Sir Robert Cecil (1563-1612), a close friend of George Calvert, was Cecil Calvert's namesake. Robert Cecil ran the government of England as King James's principal secretary of state.

From 1588 to 1603, during the last years of the reign of Queen Elizabeth I, 110 Catholics had been executed. King James I, Elizabeth's successor, enforced anti-Catholic laws to a lesser degree. Still, the 50,000 or so Catholics then in England were not free to practice their faith.

Cecil (also known as Cecilius) Calvert was born sometime in 1606, and Leonard was born about a year later. The two boys were probably George and Anne Calvert's only children, although George later had more children in his second marriage. We know little about their early life. As teenagers, both Cecil and Leonard enrolled in Oxford University.

Oxford was a frequent choice for boys of the Calverts' social standing. When Cecil and Leonard were born, their father was serving as private secretary to Sir Robert Cecil, a leading official in the court of King James I. As the boys grew up, their father's influence in the court increased. In 1617, George Calvert was knighted by the king. Two years later, he became a secretary of state and a member of the king's Privy Council. Until his resignation in 1625, he was one of the most powerful men in all of England.

Calvert left office because he was a Roman Catholic. His family had long been Catholic, but they had not openly admitted or even always practiced their Catholicism during George Calvert's rise to prominence. England was a staunchly Protestant nation in those years, and to reveal that he was a Catholic would have ruined Calvert's career. Many other Catholics who had achieved status in the early seventeenth century practiced the same caution.

Even after his retirement, George Calvert was held in high regard by the Crown. King James rewarded him for his years of service to England by giving him more land in Ireland and naming him the first Lord Baltimore.

George Calvert had long been fascinated by the idea of colonization in the New World. He was a stockholder in the Virginia Company, which had founded Jamestown, and in the Council for New England, which funded ventures in that region. In 1622, Calvert had received a grant to colonize Newfoundland in what is now Canada. He made a short visit to his land there in 1627, and he returned the next year with his second wife, Joan, all of the children except Cecil, and about 40 settlers.

The Calvert family's first experience as settlers in North America was not a happy one. "I came to build and settle and sow," complained George, "and I am fallen to fighting Frenchmen," who had rival claims to the region. What's more, the land was harsh and the winters terribly cold. After a year in Newfoundland, the family traveled south to the warmer climes of Virginia.

Lord Baltimore, however, had not given up his plans for colonizing. His original benefactor, King James, had died in 1625. Now he turned to James's son, King Charles I, pleading for a grant of land in or near Virginia. In early 1632, the king gave him a charter to the province of Carolina, south of the settled area of Virginia. When anti-Catholic Virginians protested, the king offered Lord Baltimore a different province. His new grant was for all the territory between the south bank of the Potomac River north to near where Philadelphia is now located, including present-day Delaware.

The grant gave Lord Baltimore about 10 million acres of land, which was rather small for a

George Calvert (c.1580-1632), secretly Catholic, handled diplomatic relations with Catholic Spain while he was on the Privy Council.

"From the midst of October to the midst of May, there is a sad face of winter upon all this land, both sea and land so frozen as they are not penetrable, no plant or vegetable thing appearing out of the earth until it be about the beginning of May."
—George Calvert, writing to King Charles about Newfoundland, 1628

colony in the land-rich New World. George Calvert wanted to call the new territory "Crescentia," but the king suggested "Terra Mariae"—Latin for "Mary's Land," or Maryland—in honor of his French-born queen, Henrietta Maria. Of course, the king's suggestion was followed.

George Calvert, Lord Baltimore, would not be able to settle America himself, however, for he died at about 52 years of age on April 15, 1632, before the charter for Maryland was formally issued. Just two months later, Cecil, who inherited his father's title, received the Maryland grant.

This early map of Maryland shows the region dotted with trees around Chesapeake Bay (here spelled "Chesapeack"), with Virginia to the south (left) and New England (Nova Anglia) to the north.

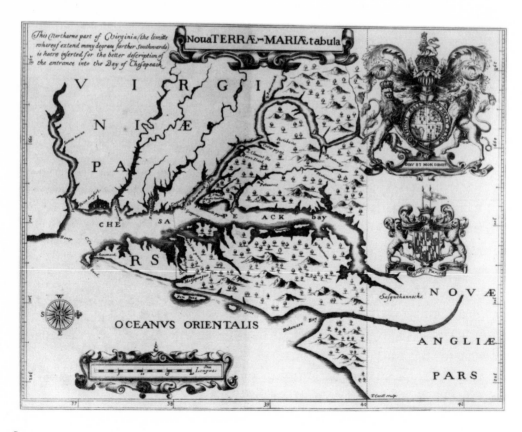

Maryland before the Calverts

An oddly shaped region straddling the northern arm of the Chesapeake Bay, Maryland was home to several Algonquin Indian tribes before the arrival of European settlers. These American Indians lived in small, widely scattered tribal villages spread along the banks of the Chesapeake Bay. Members of the Nanticoke confederacy inhabited the bay's eastern shore. On the western shore, another confederation was dominated by the Piscataways.

A whole array of Europeans landed on Maryland's shores after John Cabot first laid eyes on the area in 1498. Giovanni da Verrazano, an Italian, probably visited the region in 1524, and Spanish explorer Pedro Menéndez Marqués, nephew of Florida founder Pedro Menéndez de Avilés, explored the Chesapeake Bay for Spanish Florida about 40 years later. In the early seventeenth century, England became keen on settling the region. Bartholomew Gilbert landed in 1603. Four years later, John Smith sailed up from Jamestown and mapped the entire bay. But the land was not granted to any company or proprietor until 1632, when King Charles I awarded the area to Lord Baltimore.

The Maryland charter gave Cecil Calvert almost unlimited power as the first Lord Proprietor of Maryland—more power than any other New World proprietor. In exchange for settling the land and providing a buffer between England's Virginia colony to the south and the Dutch and Swedish colonies along the Delaware River to the north, he was made the equivalent of a feudal lord, or a king in his own little kingdom. He was granted the authority to raise an army, declare war, make laws, punish or pardon criminals, appoint officials, and distribute land as he saw fit.

Some members of the old Virginia Company were unhappy about the grant given to Cecil Calvert

The charter granted to Cecil Calvert was modeled on one given to the bishop of Durham in England in the fourteenth century. This charter made Calvert an absolute lord over his subjects, although the people of Maryland enjoyed the same legal rights as English subjects.

Cecil Calvert, second Lord Baltimore (1606-1675), appears stately looking in his middle age here, but he was just 26 years old when he inherited the title to Maryland.

and threatened legal action. The Virginia Company, a joint-stock company, had been formed in 1606 to finance the settlement of the enormous Virginia territory. When the company reorganized in 1609, it was granted land stretching all the way from Florida to New England. Although the Virginia Company had been dissolved in 1624 in the wake of charges that it had been mismanaged, members now sought to obtain a new grant to this huge tract of land.

While Cecil had planned to lead the colonists to America himself, he needed to remain in England to safeguard his charter because of the legal difficulties with the Virginia Company. In fact, he would never even visit the land given to him by the king. He did, however, actively promote the new colony.

Under Cecil Calvert's authorization, a Jesuit missionary named Father Andrew White wrote *An Account of the Colony of the Lord Baron of Baltimore* in 1633, hoping to attract colonists. Lord Baltimore offered 100 acres for each man or woman who came to help settle the colony. Wealthier colonists could receive 2,000 acres of land if they paid for the transport of five other settlers, who would work for them as indentured servants.

Since the colony of Maryland was to be a place where Catholics, particularly Catholic gentry like the Calverts, could live freely and gain wealth, Lord Baltimore also publicized the fact that the new colony guaranteed freedom of religion to all its Christian settlers. This law was to soothe the fears of Protestants as well, for English Protestants had suffered under the reign of the Catholic queen Mary a century earlier.

By mid-October 1633, about 200 colonists had been recruited and were ready to leave for Maryland. Included in this number were two Jesuit priests who were to meet the religious needs of the Catholic settlers and, it was hoped, convert the American Indians

A Jesuit is a member of a Catholic religious order known as the Society of Jesus. Founded in France in the 1530s by Saint Ignatius of Loyola, the order is noted for devotion to the Pope and for its teaching mission.

"It is acknowledged that the situation of the country is excellent and very advantageous. . . . The climate is serene and mild, not oppressively hot like that of Florida and old Virginia, nor bitterly cold like that of New England. . . . There are also vast herds of cows, and wild oxen, fit for beasts of burden and good to eat."
—*An Account of the Colony of the Lord Baron of Baltimore*

"His Lordship requires his said Governor and Commissioners . . . to preserve unity and peace amongst all the passengers on Shipboard, and that they suffer no scandal nor offense be given to any of the Protestants . . . and that the said Governor and Commissioners treat the Protestants with as much mildness and favor as Justice will permit. And this [is] to be observed at Land as well as at Sea."
—Cecil Calvert

"On the 3 of March [we] came into Chesapeake Bay, at the mouth of the Potomac. This bay is the most delightful water I ever saw, between two sweet lands. . . . [The Potomac] is the sweetest and greatest river I have seen, so that the Thames is but a little finger to it."
—Father Andrew White

who lived in the colony. About 17 of the colonists were gentry who would ultimately own large tracts of land. Most of the gentry were Catholic, while almost all of the remaining settlers were Protestant artisans, craftspeople, farmers, and indentured servants. The fact that most of the wealthy people were Catholic and most of the laborers Protestant would lead to problems in this Catholic-owned colony in later years.

As the colonists prepared to set sail from England, Cecil Calvert wrote a set of instructions for the settlers to follow in their new home. It is noteworthy that the first of the 15 instructions included in Cecil's letter dealt with religious tolerance.

On November 22, the *Ark* and the *Dove* left England. It took more than three months to cross the Atlantic, with stops to gather supplies at the Caribbean island colonies of St. Kitts and Barbados. Finally, on March 3, 1634, following a brief visit to Virginia, the ships came to anchor near present-day St. Clement's Island.

Although Cecil remained in England, his younger brother, Leonard, and half brother George led the first group of colonists. Leonard, who was named first governor of the colony by his brother, was given broad powers to oversee colonial affairs. He was in charge of military matters, appointed other government officers, called and dismissed the colonial assembly, and granted patents for lands. Leonard Calvert also served as the chief judge. The Protestant indentured servants of Maryland soon came to resent their Catholic governor's authority.

Indentured Servants

For centuries in England, land had been in short supply, and landlords with large estates owned the bulk of the country's land. Consequently, the landless population had grown. Desperately poor, with no place to raise their own food or build their own shelter, landless people could be easily exploited as cheap labor.

The British settlement of the New World changed this situation. In North America, there were not enough people to work the abundant land. Several colonies tried to enslave American Indians, but the efforts were not successful because many Indians succumbed to European diseases, and survivors easily escaped into the woods. Enslaving Indians also brought the risk of retaliation. Gradually, the English began to import Africans as slaves, but the landowners were not yet making enough money from crops to afford the expense. Not until the early eighteenth century was African slavery a significant labor source in the South.

In the seventeenth century, the English in America turned increasingly toward a new kind of labor: indentured servitude.

In exchange for transportation, poor men and women came with contracts that gave their labor to a master for a certain period, usually five or seven years. Because ship captains were paid according to the number of servants they brought, sometimes people were kidnapped or drugged and forced to sign contracts of servitude. Other times, convicted criminals were given the option of servitude or execution—often for crimes as minor as shoplifting or hunting on someone else's land.

For the duration of their servitude, these servants were actually owned by their masters. They were expected to follow orders and could be whipped for disobedience or for running away. Often they were not allowed to marry, and women could be punished for becoming pregnant.

Once their contracts were up, however, the servants were free. Usually contracts stipulated that former servants receive a plot of land, tools for working it, and clothing. Unlike slaves, who were forced to work their entire lives without reward, servants could hope to—and often did—become independent farmers and citizens.

Leonard Calvert (1607-1647), the first governor of Maryland

From the beginning of his rule in Maryland, Leonard Calvert was determined to establish peaceful relations with the Native Americans who lived in the region. Soon after the ships anchored, he and some of the other colonists made their way up the Potomac River in a small boat to a nearby Indian village. There Leonard met with the chief of the local Piscataway Indian tribe. Then he visited the chief of the Yoacomacos and purchased land for the settlement. Instead of money, Leonard gave the chief "axes, hoes, cloth and hatchets." After this meeting, the governor led the colonists to a rise on what is now known as the St. Mary's River, the place chosen as the site of the new colony. St. Mary's, the name Leonard gave the town in honor of both the Virgin Mary and the wife of King Charles I, would be the new colony's capital for more than 60 years.

St. Mary's was nearly ideal. The colonists settled into a village purchased from the Yoacomacos. Temporarily, they lived side by side with the Indians, who taught them to make bread with grains grown in fields. A newly erected mill ground the grain. What they could not grow or produce themselves, the colonists could obtain by trading with other existing English colonies. The fledgling colony was thus able to avoid the disasters that had struck Jamestown, where more than half of the first settlers had died of hunger and disease less than 30 years before.

While Cecil Calvert had promoted his new colony as a place free from religious tensions, his claim was more a dream than a reality. There was dissension on board the *Ark* and the *Dove* even

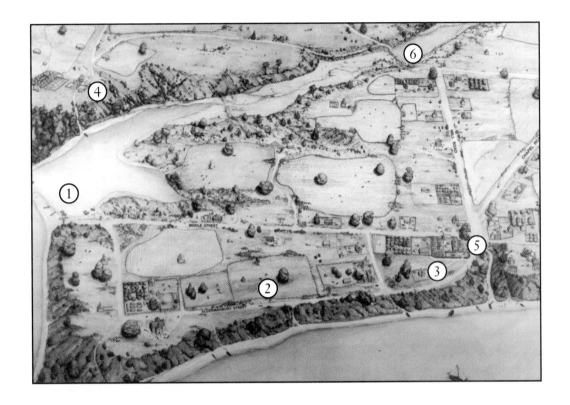

before the ships reached America and more conflict once the colony was founded. Some Protestant Virginians, hoping the Calvert colony would fail so they could stake a claim to the land, started rumors among the Indian population that the newcomers were Spaniards who had come to destroy them. Later they also tried to convince the Protestants in Maryland—most of them indentured servants—to revolt against their Catholic masters.

The major troublemaker was a man named William Claiborne. Claiborne had come to Virginia in about 1621. He had served as secretary of state there and had explored the Chesapeake Bay for that

Although Maryland's first capital has disappeared, scholars believe St. Mary's might have looked like this in 1685. Boats entered the landing at left (1). The town was spread out to allow for pastures (2) and gardens. Some of the buildings from the Calverts' time were the townhouse (3) and plantation (4) of Cecil Calvert's son Charles; Leonard Calvert's home, which was also the first State House (5); and a mill for processing grains (6).

colony. With the king's blessing, Claiborne had also established a trading post on Kent Island in the Chesapeake Bay. To Claiborne, Kent Island was in the colony of Virginia. When the Maryland grant was made to Cecil Calvert, however, that island became part of Maryland. Claiborne refused to submit to the rule of the new proprietor and challenged Calvert's right to his land.

The inhabitants of Kent Island were loyal Virginians—and Protestants. Beginning in April 1635, when Maryland seized a trading ship sailing for William Claiborne, people from Kent Island and Maryland clashed violently. Then, in February 1638, Leonard Calvert led a group of soldiers to the island. Claiborne was not there, but Leonard's men arrested his agents. The other residents of the island agreed to accept the authority of the Calverts.

In the 1640s, Maryland was wracked by even more serious conflicts. England was in the midst of a civil war between the Puritans and the Cavaliers, the Royalist supporters of King Charles I. This war soon had repercussions in Maryland, where many Puritans had settled because they were attracted by the promise of religious freedom.

The hostility began when Captain Richard Ingle got permission from the Puritan Parliament to capture the king's ships in the Chesapeake Bay. Maryland authorities, who were loyal to the king, arrested Ingle. After his release, Ingle went to England, but he returned to Maryland in early 1645. Joining forces with the still-defiant William Claiborne, Ingle captured St. Mary's and forced its

King Charles I (1600-1649) eventually lost his struggle with the Puritan-dominated Parliament in the English Civil War. He was beheaded by his enemies in 1649.

inhabitants to take an oath promising to support the Puritans. The rebels also recaptured Kent Island, returning it to Claiborne's control. Leonard Calvert was forced to take refuge in Virginia.

Captain Ingle held St. Mary's and southern Maryland for two years. But in 1647, while Ingle was in England, Leonard returned to Maryland at the head of a small army of Marylanders and Virginians. Victory was surprisingly easy. Without their leader, the rebels scattered, and the Calverts resumed control of Maryland.

Even though it was troubled, the colony grew steadily from its earliest days. Cecil Calvert continued promoting Maryland in England, printing the glowing reports sent back by his associates. More settlers came and soon pushed their way up the rivers near St. Mary's, clearing land for new plantations.

Leonard Calvert undoubtedly knew of the difficulties faced by the Virginia settlers in Jamestown and managed to avoid their mistakes. No time was wasted searching for a sea route to the East Indies or hunting for gold. Fortunately, the fertile lands around St. Mary's repaid the settlers handsomely for their planting efforts. Maryland was able to export part of its first crop, dispatching the *Dove* to Boston to trade corn, a plant introduced to them by the Indians, for fish and other supplies. Soon, tobacco became a cash crop, enriching the colony.

Leonard also turned his attention to matters of government. According to the charter, only the proprietor could propose laws, but the freemen—the adult men of the colony who were not indentured servants—had the right to give advice on the laws and to approve or reject them. When Governor Leonard Calvert called the first assembly of freemen to meet at St. Mary's in February 1635, more conflict arose. Exceeding their rights under the charter, this assembly created laws and sent them to the proprietor. After keeping the freemen waiting for more than two years, Cecil Calvert rejected this legislation in April 1637 and sent the colonists his own set of laws instead. In the assembly's next session, these laws, too, were rejected.

Maryland had now been operating for about four years without a body of laws. Leonard could govern according to the laws of England, but these did not allow for capital punishment outside of England. Since most English leaders of the time saw the death penalty as a crucial part of a legal system, this situation could not last. Finally, in 1638, Cecil agreed to allow the freemen to draft legislation. He also gave Leonard the right to approve laws until he himself had time to consider them. With these changes, the assembly passed Maryland's first body of legislation—42 bills signed into law by the governor. Despite Lord Baltimore's wishes, Maryland was well on its way to becoming a representative democracy.

Minor conflicts persisted between Catholics and Puritan Protestants, but Maryland achieved its goal of religious tolerance for all Christians during its earliest years. (Like most American colonies, Maryland did not seek to protect the right of Jews or American Indians to religious freedom.) Cecil and Leonard Calvert knew that the only way they had

any hope of winning religious freedom for Catholics was to guarantee that freedom to Protestants as well. They knew they could not make Roman Catholicism the state religion the way the Puritans had imposed their beliefs on colonists in Massachusetts.

Leonard Calvert went to extremes to avoid giving offense to Protestants. In 1641, when the Jesuits constructed a chapel at St. Mary's, he forced them to give up the building. And later, when the priests wanted to negotiate with local Native Americans to buy their own land, he stopped the negotiations.

Ultimately, however, the dream of religious toleration for all Christians proved to be just that—a dream. While the colony was intended as a refuge

This romantic painting from 1908 honors Cecil Calvert (wearing armor) for his work for peace and justice for American Indians and Maryland settlers.

for Catholics seeking freedom from persecution and aspiring to own large estates in North America, most of the people who came were poor Protestants seeking land and a chance to make a living. By about 1640, Protestants—mostly freemen with small plots of land they rented from wealthy Catholics—had virtual control of the assembly. Members of the Calvert family and their friends, however, retained most of the chief positions of leadership in the colony. For a time, leading Protestants supported the Catholic proprietor, but then the more extremist Puritans gained power.

Leonard Calvert's death on June 9, 1647, just a few months after his triumph over Richard Ingle and William Claiborne, removed the Puritan zealots' last obstacle. As in England, where the Puritan Parliament fought the Anglican monarchy, Maryland was plunged into political and religious conflict.

Cecil Calvert still attempted, in the face of rising Protestant influence in England and Maryland, to provide the freedom of religion Maryland had promised its settlers. In 1649, he sent to the colony from England the Act of Toleration, which guaranteed religious liberty to all Christians. The Act of Toleration was overturned just three years later when Puritans took control of the colonial government. By the end of 1652, anti-Catholic laws were on the books in the former Catholic haven.

Even for Puritans in England these repressive laws were too much. Oliver Cromwell, the leader of England's Puritan government, tried to make Maryland's Puritans more tolerant. Instead, the

---

Following Leonard's death, the colony was ruled by a succession of governors named by Cecil Calvert. Cecil's half brother, Philip Calvert, served for a time and was succeeded by Charles Calvert, Cecil's son, who later became the third Lord Baltimore.

Puritans in Maryland seized the government of the colony in 1655. More than two years later, in November 1657, Cromwell took action and restored the colony to Lord Baltimore. Religious liberty was reinstated, and the Puritans' tyranny of the settlers in Maryland came to an end. After putting down yet another attempted takeover by the Puritans in 1660, Cecil remained the Lord Proprietor of Maryland until he died at the age of 69 on November 30, 1675.

While political events in England made it impossible for Maryland's early settlers to experience true religious freedom, Cecil and Leonard Calvert had brought their father's dream to life by becoming the first colonial founders to attempt to put the principle of freedom of conscience into practice in America. At Cecil's death, Maryland enjoyed a robust economy based on tobacco and had a stable government under the leadership of Cecil's son, Governor Charles Calvert, the third Lord Baltimore.

Oliver Cromwell (1599-1658) was the dictatorial ruler of England after the Puritans defeated King Charles I in the English Civil War. He called for Charles's execution and destroyed Irish resistance to English rule. Although he claimed to support religious tolerance, he usually showed little for Anglicans, Catholics, and Quakers.

Maryland after the Calverts

The Calverts lost possession of Maryland several times. Although 30 years of relative peace followed the restoration of Maryland to the family in 1657, the Crown assumed control in 1688, and the king and queen made Maryland a royal province four years later. After 1688, Anglicanism became the official religion in Maryland. The Calverts regained control in 1715, but the family never again enjoyed the wide range of powers held by Cecil and Leonard Calvert.

The city of Baltimore was founded in 1729 and grew to dominate the colony's economy as the port city for the tobacco trade. Abandoned in the 1690s, St. Mary's has disappeared without a trace.

Maryland was one of the first colonies to resist British rule. Marylanders had their own version of a "tea party" in 1774 when colonists set fire to the *Peggy Stewart*, a ship carrying excessively taxed tea, in Annapolis harbor. On July 3, 1776, the state assembly disavowed allegiance to the king. Four months later, Maryland became the first of the former colonies to adopt a state constitution. Its residents were active in both Continental Congresses and several were signers of the Declaration of Independence.

In 1752, Baltimore, now Maryland's largest city, had only about 300 residents. Even then, the town's economy was based around its harbor.

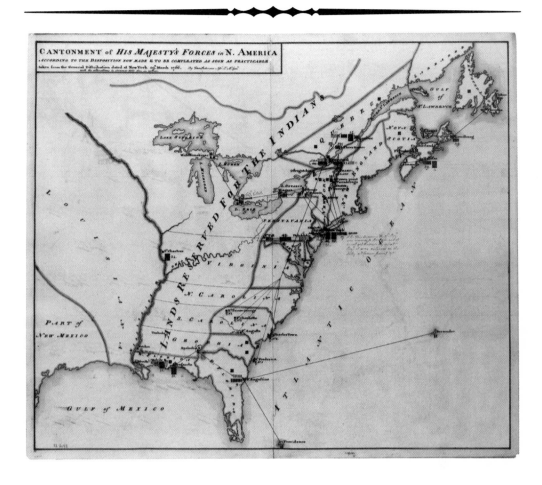

This 1766 military map of the English colonies shows Maryland tucked between the larger colonies of Virginia and Pennsylvania. Its borders remain roughly the same today.

In 1788, Maryland became the seventh state to ratify the U.S. Constitution. Three years later, the state gave the new nation about 70 square miles of land along the Potomac River for building the District of Columbia.

During the Civil War, Maryland, a slave state, was occupied by Union forces to prevent its secession. The state was the site of fierce battles, including the bloody Battle of Antietam in September 1862.

The Tangled History of Delaware

Few colonies could boast as complicated a history as Delaware, which at various times was claimed by the Dutch colony of New Netherland (later New York); the Swedish colony of New Sweden; and two English colonies, Pennsylvania and Maryland.

Home to the Algonquin Delaware Indians, the slim piece of land stretched along the western banks of the Delaware Bay and Delaware River. Henry Hudson, sailing for the Dutch East India Company

Peter Minuit (c.1580-1638) never got a chance to build New Sweden because he was lost at sea in a hurricane shortly after the colony was founded.

Henry Hudson (d. 1611) was trying to find the Northwest Passage through the continent when he explored Delaware Bay.

in 1609, was the first to enter Delaware Bay. A year later, English captain Samuel Argall sailed by and named a point Cape La Warre after Lord De la Warr, the governor of Virginia. The name and eventually the English claim would stand the test of time.

In 1631, Dutch colonists built the first European settlement in the Delaware area. Swanendael was erected on the present-day site of Lewes, Delaware, and Fort Nassau defended the eastern bank of the Delaware River in what is now New Jersey further north. Peter Minuit erected Fort Christina for New Sweden in 1638 on the site of today's Wilmington, Delaware. The Dutch were furious, but they did not manage to drive out the Swedes until 1655.

Even then, Delaware's ownership was still not established. When the English seized New Netherland in 1664 and made it New York, Dutch outposts in Delaware came with the colony. The duke of York, owner of New York, later granted Delaware to Pennsylvania in 1682. Delaware's three counties thus became the Three Lower Counties of Pennsylvania. Then the trouble with Maryland began.

Although Dutch and Swedish colonists had begun settling Delaware first, the English government claimed the Delaware territory as part of its original "Virginia" territory. The land grant to Cecil Calvert in 1632 included this land. The Calverts were locked up in court for years in their land dispute with William Penn. Delaware residents were uneasy about being subject to outside control, but they finally accepted Penn's charter in 1701—with the understanding that they could have a separate representative government.

After Americans declared their independence from England in 1776, Delaware

William Penn (1644-1718) had planned to live in his colony of Pennsylvania, but his legal battle with the Calverts took him back to England and he was never able to make a permanent home in the New World.

became separate from Pennsylvania, and in 1787 it was the first state to ratify the U.S. Constitution. Even though it was a slave state, Delaware's northern ties could be observed during the Civil War, when it remained loyal to the Union.

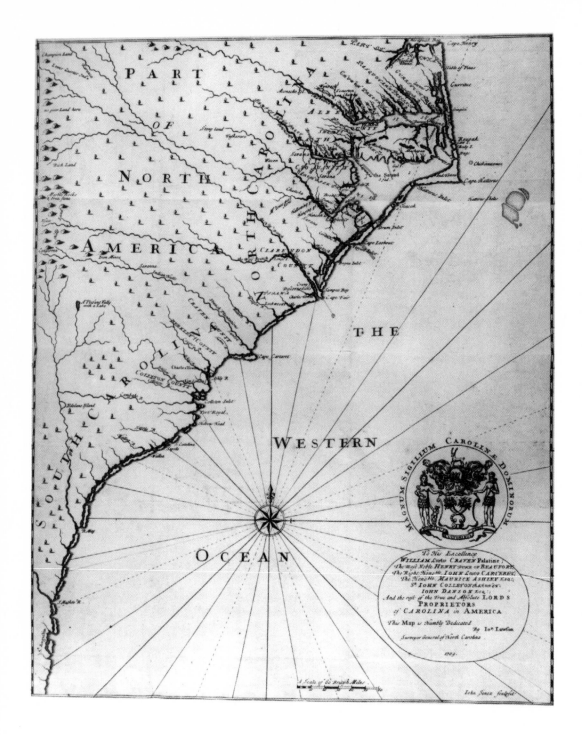

Chapter Five

Henry Woodward
and the
Settlement of the Carolinas

On May 29, 1664, a party of about 800 English settlers stepped ashore on Cape Fear in what is now the state of North Carolina. These people had come from the crowded West Indian island of Barbados to the untamed shores of America in search of land for crops.

One of these Carolina settlers was an 18-year-old planter and trader named Henry Woodward. Woodward is one of many pioneer founders of America's earliest colonial history whose exploits and accomplishments are virtually unknown to all but a few historians. We know that Woodward was born sometime around 1646, and it is thought that he was a native of Barbados, one of the beautiful tropical islands in the Antilles chain that stretches in a gentle curve from the coast of Venezuela to Puerto Rico.

No picture exists of Henry Woodward, who explored the region covered by this 1709 map and beyond, into the continent's Indian territories.

John Berkeley (1602-1678), one of Lords Proprietors of the Carolinas, did most of the work recruiting the five English aristocrats who joined him, his brother William Berkeley, and John Colleton.

King Charles II (1630-1685), who regained power for the monarchy in 1660, was eager to reward the men who had supported the Crown in the English Civil War.

By the time of Woodward's birth, Barbados was a well-established English colony in the West Indies. First settled by the English in 1627, it was a major producer of sugar cane. The fertile soil of Barbados attracted so many settlers that by the 1650s people were looking for new lands to colonize. To meet this need, three large planters from Barbados decided in late 1662 that they should try to get a grant for a proprietary colony similar to Maryland in the region between Spanish Florida and English Virginia. The planters did not have enough money to finance such a colony by themselves, so they approached other powerful and wealthy men in England and enlisted their help. Early in 1663, eight men, who were known as the Lords Proprietors of Carolina, were granted a charter by King Charles II in reward for their loyalty. That same year, a party went to explore the coastal lands near Cape Fear to find a site for settlement.

The colonists who came to the Carolinas in 1664, including young Henry Woodward, cleared land for plantations and homes along the banks of what is now the Cape Fear River, about 30 miles upstream from Cape Fear. They called the waterway the Charles River in honor of their king. The next year, a second group of settlers arrived. More homes were built, land was cleared, and crops—including corn and tobacco, as well as a variety of experimental crops—were planted. By 1666, the settlement appeared to be on its way to permanence. A tract proclaiming its progress was published in London. The first settlers, the pamphlet assured prospective

colonists, had "cleared the way for those that come after, who will find good houses to be in while their own are in building; good forts to secure them from their enemies; and many things brought from other parts there."

The charter granted to the eight Carolina proprietors was similar to the one Cecil Calvert, the founder of Maryland, had received. It bestowed broad powers on the Lords Proprietors, almost like those of a king. The document gave them control of a vast territory: all the land between Albemarle Sound on the north and what is now the border between Florida and Georgia on the south.

The original Carolina settlement at Cape Fear would be abandoned. When this photograph was taken in the 1800s, the 200-year-old buildings were in ruins.

The Settlement of the Carolinas

About 30 different Native American tribes were in the Carolinas when Europeans first arrived in the area. The major groups in what is now North Carolina were the Cherokees, Catawbas, and Tuscaroras. The Cherokees and Catawbas also lived in what is now South Carolina, along with the Yamasee tribe. The Iroquoian-speaking Tuscaroras and Cherokees were fierce warriors who would resist the white settlers. The Catawbas, members of the Sioux-speaking group of tribes, would be peaceful for the most part. The Yamasees, one of the Muskogean family of tribes, would be friendly in the colonists' earliest days in the Carolinas.

During the sixteenth century, the Carolina coastline was the site of the earliest European attempts to establish colonies on the Atlantic seaboard of North America. The Spanish were the first to try. In 1526, they established a colony that lasted just a few months. The French followed, building a small settlement called Port Royal on Parris Island in today's South Carolina. Spaniards sailed up from Florida and drove out the French, founding their own colonial town of Santa Elena just north of the former French colony. In the 1580s, the English tried to found a settlement at Roanoke Island off the coast of present-day North Carolina.

The English made their claim to the territory official in 1629. Named Carolina (after the Latin word for Charles), the land was granted by King Charles I to Robert Heath, his attorney-general, in 1629. King Charles I also briefly granted the northern section of what is now North Carolina to George Calvert, Lord Baltimore, in 1632, but Virginians' complaints led him to substitute the grant of Maryland.

For the next 30 years, the region was left largely in the hands of its Indian inhabitants. The only European visitors were explorers, hunters, and a few traders.

One of the main reasons the Carolinas had not been settled was geographical. The coastline is guarded by a series of sand reefs and barrier islands, and the waters inside those reefs and islands are too shallow to allow large ships close to shore. In addition, the region was dangerously close to Spanish Florida. A new colony might have had difficulty defending itself.

Still, by the mid-1600s, interest in the region was growing. English settlements along the James River in Virginia and in the West Indies were becoming more and more crowded, and land-hungry planters looked to the vast area between Virginia and Florida.

This interest led Sir John Colleton, Sir William Berkeley, and Lord John Berkeley to plan a settlement in Carolina. In late 1662, these men, along with five of the most powerful men in England—Lord Anthony Ashley Cooper; Edward Hyde, the earl of Clarendon; George Monck, the duke of Albemarle; Sir George Carteret; and Lord Craven—applied for a grant modeled on the one given to Calvert. This grant was issued in March 1663.

These eight men, together known as the Lords Proprietors of the Carolinas, were given a huge parcel of land running from near the Florida border on the south

George Carteret (c.1610-1680) was given not only the proprietorship of the Carolinas, but also, with John Berkeley, the proprietorship of New Jersey. He and Berkeley oversaw a huge amount of American territory.

Edward Hyde (1609-1674), one of King Charles II's most trusted advisors while the Puritans controlled England, was rewarded with the title earl of Clarendon when Charles came to the throne.

all the way north to Albemarle Sound and from the Atlantic to the Pacific Oceans. The granting of the proprietary charter set the stage for colonizing the Carolinas.

The proprietors' main role was funding and promoting the colonization. In a 1666 pamphlet, they boasted, "Doubtless there is no Plantation that ever the English went upon, in all respects, so good as this."

George Monck (1608-1670), duke of Albemarle, was immortalized in the names of Albemarle Sound and the town of Albemarle, North Carolina.

Two years after Carolina's original charter was granted, it was extended to include the region of north Florida between its border and what is now the city of Daytona Beach. That meant the Carolina colony now included—according to the English government—the Spanish city of St. Augustine, which had been founded by Pedro Menéndez de Avilés in 1565.

For some years, Virginians had been relocating to the northernmost regions of the Carolina territory, while settlers from New England and Barbados settled around Cape Fear. The matter of a government for Carolina was complicated by the fact that the earliest settlers came from different places, and each of these groups had different ideas about how the government should be established. In the colony's earliest days, however, the territory was divided into three counties: Albemarle in the north and Clarendon and Craven in the south. Eventually, Albemarle would become North Carolina, while Clarendon and Craven became South Carolina. Each county had its own government, and religious freedom was guaranteed throughout Carolina.

During the earliest years of slow and halting settlement, Henry Woodward must have been only a minor figure in the colony, for his name is not mentioned in any of the surviving reports of activities at Cape Fear. That changed, however, in 1666. In that year, when he was about 20, Woodward accompanied Robert Sandford, an official of Clarendon County, on an expedition to explore the area around Port Royal in what is now South Carolina. On that mission, he worked as a "chirurgeon," or surgeon, indicating that at some time in his life he'd had at least a smattering of schooling.

At present-day Edisto Island, Woodward and the others came into contact with a group of American Indians, probably Kiawah (pronounced as "Keewah") Indians. These people had seen Europeans before, so friendly relations were quickly established, and the Indians agreed to serve as guides. More than once, in fact, they carried Sandford on their shoulders across "creeks and plashy corners of marshes." When their party reached the harbor where Charleston is now, Sandford knew the region was ideal for settlement.

Even before leaving Cape Fear, Sandford had determined that "if I liked the Country I might prevail with the Indians to let one of their nation go with me, I leaving an Englishman . . . for the mutual learning [of] their language." When the time came for the party to return to Cape Fear, Woodward volunteered to stay with the Native Americans. He

Surgeons in Woodward's time were not the highly paid professionals they are today. Woodward's work was probably much like this mid-1500s battlefield surgeon, who is extracting a spear-point from a wounded soldier.

knew this experience would be invaluable to the proprietors. Pleased, Sandford awarded Henry Woodward with "formal possession of the whole country to hold as tenant" for as long as the Lords Proprietors wished.

Sandford planned for Woodward to remain with the Indians until the English returned to pick him up. But soon after the party left, Woodward was captured by a group of Spaniards, probably soldiers from St. Augustine who had been told of his presence in the Indian village.

Woodward was taken to the old Spanish city, where he lived for about two years under a kind of house arrest. During that time, the young man managed to gain the trust of the Spaniards. Woodward converted to Roman Catholicism and was made the city's official surgeon. He knew the information he learned about the Spanish might later be of great value to his colony.

At that time, St. Augustine was, for all practical purposes, the only Spanish settlement on the eastern seaboard. Steady colonization by the English to the north and by the French in the lower Mississippi valley had forced the Spanish into a situation of simply trying to hold on to their small corner of the New World.

On May 9, 1668, an English pirate named Robert Searle made a daring raid on St. Augustine. He and his men stole ashore and attacked at night, killing about 60 Spanish settlers and looting the town. When Searle sailed away, he took Woodward with him.

Woodward stayed with Searle for more than a year as the ship's surgeon. In August 1669, they were shipwrecked in a hurricane off the coast of the Caribbean island of Nevis, but Woodward survived. Later that year, he was finally able to obtain passage on a ship bound for the Carolina colony.

By the time Woodward returned in 1670, the colony at Cape Fear had been abandoned. But Lord Anthony Ashley Cooper (or Lord Ashley) had not given up on the Carolinas. He turned his attention to the region in the south that had been explored by the Sandford party in 1666. In 1670, colonists established a settlement 25 miles inland on the Ashley River (named for Lord Ashley), well to the north of the old French settlement at Port Royal. At Lord Ashley's request, philosopher John Locke had written the colony's Fundamental Constitutions in 1669. This constitution was terribly old-fashioned, including generous land grants for plantations with feudal lords. Still, it allowed landholdings and a voice in the government to most male settlers.

Upon his return to the brand-new English colony, Woodward put his knowledge of the land and the natives to good use. He first traveled west and north on an eight-day journey to the Wateree, a branch of the Santee River. There, he established peaceful relations with the Native Americans and traded for furs. Some weeks later, when the settlement was in dire need of food, Woodward was able to obtain needed supplies from the Indians.

For the next several years, Woodward continued to travel. He went to Virginia in search of gold

"I have discovered a Country so delicious & fruitful that were it cultivated . . . it would prove a second Paradise."
—Henry Woodward to Governor John Yeamans, describing the land on the Wateree River

on orders of Lord Ashley, and he also continued to make trade agreements with the Kiawah and the Lower Creek tribes.

In 1674, Woodward undertook one of his most dangerous journeys, traveling alone to visit the village of the warlike Westo tribe on the Savannah River. That autumn, some Westos had appeared at Anthony Ashley Cooper's plantation to sell furs. Acting as Lord Ashley's special agent, Woodward met them and agreed to go to their village. His journey took him from the Ashley River settlement to the site of present-day Augusta, Georgia. For 10 days, Woodward remained a guest of the Westo tribe in their well-defended town.

Woodward's mission was crucial to the future success of South Carolina. He established peace with the Westos and reached an agreement on trade as well. In exchange for English goods, the Indians provided deerskins and fur. The Westos also sold Indian captives to the English as slaves. This association would help to make South Carolina's future capital, Charleston, the largest and wealthiest trading center in North America. Woodward's efforts opened trails that were later used by traders traveling to the Creek, Cherokee, and Chickasaw Indians living in the colony's interior. Later, these trails would lead settlers inland from the Atlantic coastline.

In the years following Woodward's visit to the Westos, the Indians were more than trading partners. They were also allies in the English efforts to drive the Spanish out of coastal Georgia, which was then considered a part of Carolina by the English.

"The chief of the Indians made long speeches intimating . . . their desire of friendship with us. This night first having oiled my eyes and joints with bear's oil, they presented me [with] deer skins, setting before me sufficient of their food to satisfy at least a half a dozen of their own appetites."
—Woodward on the Westo Indians

Using arms supplied by Woodward, Westo Indians made a series of raids on Spanish forts and missions, giving the English a foothold in the region.

The Lords Proprietors' trading monopoly with the Westos and other inland tribes benefited the proprietors at the expense of ordinary settlers. Many of the colonists resented not being able to make trades themselves. In 1680, the Ashley River settlement was moved to the junction of the Ashley and Cooper Rivers, and the capital city of Charles Town was founded. Tired of Westo raids on other Indians who lived close to Charles Town, the colonists soon

This 1727 map of "Carolana" has the colony stretching across North America beyond the Mississippi River. The region that is now North and South Carolina is actually scrunched into current Georgia and Florida in this inaccurate representation.

Named in honor of King Charles II, Charles Town was later shortened to Charleston. The Charleston waterfront, pictured here in the 1730s, has retained much of its charm.

encouraged the nearby Savannah Indians to wage war on the Westos. By 1684, only about 50 Westos remained alive, and those survivors were soon absorbed by other tribes.

While the war with the Westos must have been disturbing to Woodward, it served the colonists' purposes by breaking the proprietors' trade monopoly with the inland tribes and spurring further exploration and settlement in the interior. Once again, it was Henry Woodward, then in his late thirties, who led the way. In 1682, he had secured from the proprietors an extraordinary commission to explore the interior of Carolina beyond the Savannah River. Woodward began trading with Lower Creek Indians as far away as the Chattahoochee River, the modern-day border between Georgia and Alabama.

At Coweta, a village of the Ochese tribe, Woodward made a final trading agreement in the summer of 1685. This was to be his last visit to the interior of Carolina, for he fell ill on the trip. Near death, Woodward was carried back to Charles Town the next year, trailed by 150 Indians carrying furs. The great explorer died soon after his return.

Henry Woodward was not the founder of a particular colony or settlement. His journeys of exploration and trade, however, helped the settlement of Charles Town become a reality and opened much of the interior of the southeastern frontier to later colonization. One scholar called Henry Woodward "the pioneer . . . of English expansion in the lower south." Not only was Woodward "the first English settler in South Carolina," he was also "the first interpreter and Indian agent, the first Englishman to penetrate the western wilderness beyond the Chattahoochee." Without his efforts, the soon-to-be wealthy and powerful colony of South Carolina might not have survived.

CAROLINA;

OR A

DESCRIPTION

OF THE

PRESENT STATE OF THAT COUNTRY,

AND

THE NATURAL EXCELLENCIES THEROF;

NAMELY,

THE HEALTHFULNESS OF THE AIR, PLEASANTNESS OF THE PLACE, ADVANTAGES AND USEFULNESS OF THOSE RICH COMMODITIES THERE PLENTIFULLY ABOUNDING, WHICH MUCH ENCREASE AND FLOURISH BY THE INDUSTRY OF THE PLANTERS THAT DAILY ENLARGE THAT COLONY.

PUBLISHED BY T. A. Gent.

Cl'rk on board his Majesties Ship the Richmond,

WHICH WAS SENT OUT IN THE YEAR 1680, WITH PARTICULAR INSTRUCTIONS TO ENQUIRE INTO THE STATE OF THAT COUNTRY BY HIS MAJESTIES SPECIAL COMMAND, AND RETURN'D THIS PRESENT YEAR, 1682.

LONDON,
Printed for W. C. and to be Sold by Mrs. Grover, in Pelican Court, in Little Britain, 1682.

While Woodward continued to open new trading routes, promoters in England kept writing about the wonders of the Carolinas, as in this 1682 pamphlet.

South Carolina's Agricultural Bounty

While many of the technological contributions of Africans to North America remain hidden to history, the astounding success of rice as a cash crop in South Carolina was due to Africans' expertise in the planting and processing of this plant. The names of the men and women who introduced these successful techniques to the colony are not known, but we can still honor their efforts.

Rice was one of many crops planters in the Carolinas attempted to grow in the first decades of settlement. But the growers were inexperienced with the plant, and they failed to master the techniques necessary for its successful cultivation. Then they turned to their slaves for help.

For centuries, people from the west coast of Africa, especially present-day Sierra Leone and Ghana, had grown rice in fields carefully flooded and drained to create the proper growing conditions. They had also perfected methods of efficiently drying the harvested crop and removing the hull that covered the grains of rice.

Slave sale records show that planters paid premium prices for slaves from the rice-growing regions because they needed their knowledge. In the years after 1695, when planters began to import slaves from Africa's rice-growing areas in large numbers, rice became South Carolina's first profitable crop. Rice variety names like

These women hulling rice in the early 1900s used centuries-old techniques brought to South Carolina by their West African ancestors.

"Carolina gold" show how valuable the plant was to the young colony's economy.

Indigo, which could be used to make a valuable blue-colored dye, was another tricky plant to cultivate. It had failed in South Carolina until the efforts of Eliza Lucas Pinckney. Elizabeth Lucas, always called Eliza, was born in about 1722 in Antigua, one of the English colonies in the

West Indies. She came to South Carolina in 1738 when her father inherited three rice plantations.

Only a few months after moving to South Carolina, George Lucas was called back to Antigua to become lieutenant governor. Sixteen-year-old Eliza was left in charge of the three plantations: one on the Combahee River; one on the Waccamaw River; and a third—where Eliza lived with her mother and sister—on the Wappoo, a small creek that connected the Ashley and Stono Rivers near Charleston.

Not long after her father's departure from South Carolina, violence erupted between Spain and England. The War of Jenkins's Ear, as it was called, blocked rice shipments—virtually the only crop in the colony at that time—from leaving the colony. Planters needed alternate crops to avoid financial ruin, so Eliza's father began sending her packets of a variety of seeds from Antigua to plant on his plantations.

Eliza had loved botany, or the study of

The indigo plant

plants, since she was a young girl. By 1740, the 18-year-old was experimenting with various crops, including ginger and alfalfa. In 1741, she tried indigo. A plant native to the West Indies, indigo was used to make fabric dyes that England could then only buy from France. Indigo had the potential to be very profitable. Although Carolina planters had already tried to plant and cultivate it without success, Eliza believed indigo could be grown in South Carolina's rich soil.

Her work plagued by early frosts and grasshoppers, it took three years of experimenting to harvest a decent crop. Finally, in 1744, Eliza was ready to produce the indigo dye. This process used three connecting vats. In the first, indigo leaves were steeped like tea bags in hot water. The liquid drained from the first vat was stirred with paddles in the second so the solids could separate. Then the liquid was drained into the third and smallest container, where the solid material was allowed to settle.

When it dried, it became what the planters soon called "blue gold."

The dye-maker instructing Eliza came from the Caribbean island of Montserrat, where indigo was an important source of revenue. Apparently to protect that island's indigo trade, he sabotaged Eliza's first efforts. But Eliza Lucas Pinckney, who had recently married, fired him and still managed to perfect the process without him.

Indigo was planted on much of the highland in South Carolina the next year, while the lowlands along the rivers and tidal estuaries were still devoted to rice crops. In 1750, 63,000 pounds of indigo were exported to England. Five years later, exports of indigo products amounted to more than 1 million pounds per year. Indigo had become a cash crop even more important to the colony than rice.

As she continued experimenting, Eliza also raised a family. Two of her sons, Charles Cotesworth Pinckney and Thomas Pinckney, were Revolutionary War heroes. When Eliza Lucas Pinckney died in 1793, President George Washington asked to be a pallbearer at her funeral. He later described her as one of the country's greatest heroines.

The Carolinas from Colonies to Statehood

The Lords Proprietors profited little from settling North and South Carolina. During the proprietary period, England was comparatively stable, and few people wanted to emigrate to the wilds of the frontier.

The colony's growth was also slowed by frequent and bloody conflicts between settlers and American Indians. While Henry Woodward's treaties brought peace for a time, violence was inevitable as the English pushed into Indian territories. After destructive wars with the Tuscarora Indians in the north (1711-1713) and the Yamasee Indians in the south (1715-1716), native resistance was weakened. But white settlers did not completely drive out the Indians until the 1830s.

The government also evolved in this period. North and South Carolina were considered separate colonies by 1691, with a deputy governor, named by the South Carolina governor, serving in North Carolina. By 1712, there were separate governors.

In 1729, King George II took control of North and South Carolina and made them royal colonies. The only major settlements then were located at Charleston and around Albemarle Sound. Under the leadership of a succession of royal governors, the number of residents jumped from about 35,000 in 1729 to almost 350,000 in 1775. At the same time, both North and South Carolina became more prosperous, with slaves harvesting bounty crops of tobacco, cotton, rice, and indigo.

North and South Carolina resisted English rule early in their histories. North Carolinians unsuccessfully rebelled against the proprietors in 1677 and 1708. The South Carolina assembly was writing its own laws by 1693. Upset by the proprietors' failure to provide defense against the Indians, settlers there overthrew proprietary rule in 1719 and sought military aid from the king instead. People in both South and North Carolina were leaders in resistance to British rule in the years before the Revolutionary War.

The first colony to declare its independence, North Carolina furnished 10 regiments to the Continental army. On May 23, 1788, South Carolina became the eighth state to ratify the U.S. Constitution. North Carolina, on November 21, 1789, was the twelfth of the 13 original states to ratify the U.S. Constitution.

The wealth of the Carolinas was built on the backs of enslaved Africans, who formed the majority of the population in South Carolina by the early 1700s. In this illustration, slaves are sold at an auction in Charleston.

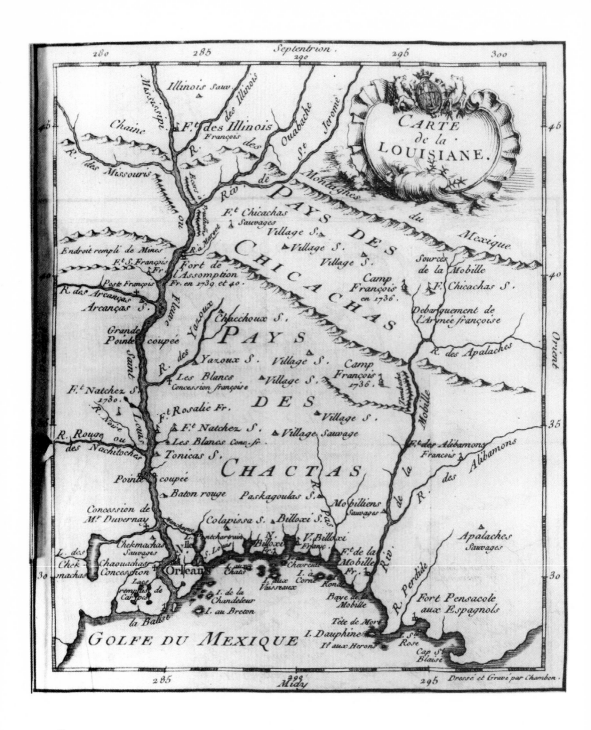

CARTE
de la
LOUISIANE.

Septentrion.

280   285   290   295   300

46   46

Mississipi   Illinois Sauv.

Chaine   F.t des Illinois   R. des Illinois

R. des Missouris   François   des   Ouabache

Riv.   S.t Jerôme

Montagnes   du   Mexique

PAYS DES

F.t Chicachas S.   Sources
Sauvages   de la Mobile

Endroit rempli de Mines   Village S.
F.t S. François   Fort de   Village S.   F. Chicachas S.
Fr.   l'Assomption   Camp
Poste François   Fr. en 1739 et 40.   François   Debarquement de
R. des Arcanças   en 1736.   L'Armée françoise
Arcanças S.   Chacchoux S.
Grande   PAYS
Pointe coupée   R. des   Yazoux S. Village S.   Camp   R. des Apalaches
Yazoux S.   Village S.   François
Les Blancs   Village S.   1736.
F.t Natchez S.   Concession françoise   Mobille
1730.   DES
R. Noire   F.t Rosalie Fr.   Village S.
R. Rouge ou   F.t Natchez S.   Village Sauvage
des Nachitoches   Les Blancs Conc. fr.   F.t des Alibamons
Tonicas S.   François
CHACTAS   R. des   Alibamons
Pointe
coupée   Baton rouge   Paskagoulas S.
Concession de   Mobilliens
M.r Duvernay   Colapissa S. Biloxi S.   Sauvages
L. Pontchartrain
Chekmachas   S.t Louis   N.   V. Biloxi   Apalaches
Sauvages   Biloxi   Françe   Sauvages
Chek-   Chaouachas   Chavrente   F.t de la   Riv.
machas   Concession   Orleans   L. à   Mobille
I. aux   Fr.
Lacs   I. de la   Vaisseaux   I. à   Fort Pensacole
remplis de   Chandeleur   Ronde   R. Perdide   aux Espagnols
Carpes.   I. au Breton   Baye de   30
la Balise   Mobille   Cap S.t
Tête de Mort   Blaise
GOLFE DU MEXIQUE   I. Dauphine   S.te
I.s aux Herons   Rose

285   290   295   Dressé et Gravé par Chambon.
Midy

118

Chapter Six

---◆---

Iberville & Bienville
and the
Founding of French Louisiana

---◆---

In March 1699, two small boats sailed southwest along the coast of the Gulf of Mexico, 80 miles south of present-day New Orleans. The boats, trading vessels of a type called *traversiers* by the French, were part of a fleet sent by the king of France to establish a colony near the mouth of the Mississippi River. The fleet was under the command of 37-year-old Pierre le Moyne d'Iberville, a well-known sailor and a hero of the recent battles between French and British fur-trading companies in Canada. Accompanying Iberville, as he is usually known, was his 19-year-old brother, Jean Baptiste le Moyne de Bienville, generally called Bienville.

The two boats had threaded their way among scores of tiny islands during several days of storm-tossed sailing. Finally, Iberville spied a narrow break

This early French map of Louisiana (covering territory from Illinois on the north to Florida in the southeast) shows settlements and forts established by Iberville and Bienville. They include Fort Rosalie and Fort Natchez along the Mississippi, New Orleans near the river's delta, Biloxi (here "Billoxi") further east, and Mobile ("Mobille") by Mobile Bay. Many regions and towns are identified by their Native American inhabitants, such as Pays des Chactas (Choctaw country).

Jean Baptiste le Moyne de Bienville (1680-1768), at left, acquired his surname after the death of one of his brothers, François, sieur (sir) de Bienville, in 1691. This title, like that of Pierre le Moyne d'Iberville (1661-1706), at right, had been given to François by his father in honor of a region of France.

in the shoreline. He quickly turned his boat. Pushed by the strong breeze, the vessel sped through the opening and into calm water. Iberville, Bienville, and the others in the party had entered the Mississippi River through the mouth of what is now known as the North Pass. Soon they would establish a French settlement on the Gulf of Mexico.

In July 1661, Pierre le Moyne was born in Montreal, Canada. He was the third son of 14 children, including 11 sons, who were born to Charles le Moyne and his wife, Catherine. Pierre's brother Jean Baptiste, born on February 23, 1680, was the couple's eighth son.

Charles le Moyne, one of Montreal's early pioneers, had become one of Canada's wealthiest men. Pierre, Jean Baptiste, and the other le Moyne children undoubtedly enjoyed all the advantages that money could buy on the French Canadian frontier. This did not mean, however, that the family lived in luxury, for Montreal in those days was a rough-and-tumble village of about 40 houses. The dirt streets became clogged with mud in the spring. To defend against frequent Indian attacks, a tall palisade of pointed logs surrounded the village.

At about the age of 12, seven years before Jean Baptiste's birth, Pierre left home to begin a life of adventure. For the next decade, he served as a midshipman in the French navy, learning navigation, seamanship, and the art of waging war. Then, probably in about 1683, Pierre met a man who would spark his fascination to discover new worlds. Robert Cavelier de La Salle, a French adventurer, had just completed his exploration of the Mississippi River for France, descending the river to its mouth at the Gulf of Mexico. Now Pierre also became interested in the possibility of founding a French colony at the mouth of that great river.

During these years, the French and English were engaged in a competition for control of the valuable fur trade in Canada. This struggle between the Hudson's Bay Company, a trading company established by the British in 1670, and the French Company of the North, a trading company chartered by the French government in 1682, often erupted into open warfare.

Réné Robert Cavelier, sieur de La Salle

Born in France on November 21, 1643, Robert de La Salle went to Canada in 1667. The explorer dreamed of finding a route to the Pacific through the North American interior. Leaving Peoria, Illinois, to search for this passageway in 1682, he explored the Mississippi River from the present-day site of St. Louis, Missouri, to the river's mouth at the Gulf of Mexico (see map below). Before this mission, French territory was limited to Canada and the Great Lakes region. French Louisiana, named in honor of King Louis XIV, stretched from Illinois south to the Gulf, and from Florida in the southeast to the territory of New Spain in the American Southwest.

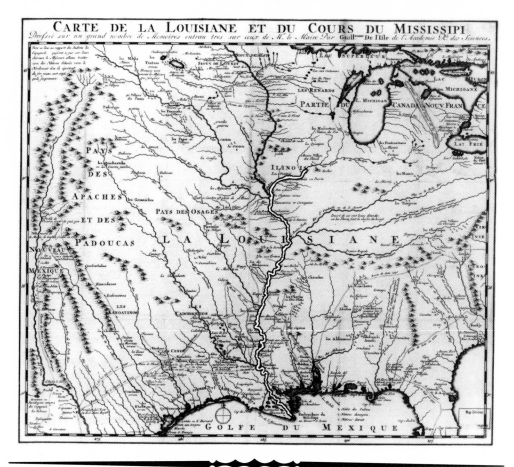

Fiercely patriotic, Pierre hated the English. In the years between 1686 and 1697, he earned a reputation as a brave and merciless naval officer as he led raids on English trading posts on Canada's Hudson Bay, in Newfoundland, on the St. Lawrence River, and in New York and Maine. In his last battle in 1697, Pierre defeated the much larger English man-of-war, the 56-gun *Hampshire*, while commanding the *Pelican*, a warship with only 44 guns.

Pierre's brother Jean Baptiste was at his side in the defeat of the *Hampshire*. The younger le Moyne had followed in his brother's footsteps by becoming a sailor at the age of 12, serving under Pierre from the start of his naval career. Not long after the *Pelican*'s successful battle, Jean Baptiste was seriously wounded in a raid on a British fort. But the young man recovered to help his brother create a more lasting monument to France in what is now the southern United States.

After hostilities between the English and French in Canada ended with a peace treaty in 1697, the French government turned its attention to the region around the mouth of the Mississippi River. A French colony there would thwart Spanish designs on the North American continent by dividing their land in Florida from their territory in the Southwest. It would also serve as a barrier to the English, who were already expanding their landholdings westward from the Atlantic seaboard. Taking control of the Mississippi River would also be valuable for trade. Furs trapped further north could be shipped from there to Europe.

French Louisiana before Settlement

Native Americans were living in the region the French called Louisiana—including the modern-day states of Alabama, Mississippi, and Louisiana—at least 8,000 years before the first Europeans visited the territory.

The natives living in the western part of the French territory (today's Louisiana) were, for the most part, hunter-gatherers, subsisting by hunting game in the forests, fishing in the rivers and streams, and foraging for wild grains, nuts, and berries. About 2,000 years ago, some of these Indians became farmers, planting corn, squash, beans, sunflowers, and other crops on floodplains along the region's many rivers.

Many of the American Indian peoples in Louisiana may have migrated there long ago from Central America. Louisiana's tribal and language groups were the Caddos in the northwest, the Tunicas in the northeast, the Natchez in the middle of Louisiana's present borders, the Atakapas in the southwest, and the Chitimachas in the south. Tribes east of the Mississippi River spoke Muskogean. When Iberville and Bienville made their way up the Mississippi, there were an estimated 15,000 Indians living in the region they explored.

The Natchez Indians were one of the few surviving tribes of a once-flourishing Temple Mound culture that built huge earthen temples for religious worship. The Natchez people called their earthly ruler the "Great Sun."

The eastern region of the French territory, located along the Gulf of Mexico (now the states of Mississippi and Alabama), was home to a half-dozen major tribes, most of whom spoke Muskogean languages. The Chickasaws lived in the north, and the Choctaws, Natchez, and Sioux-speaking Biloxis and Pascagoulas lived in the south. Like their counterparts to the west, these Indians were generally peaceful people who spent much of their time hunting, fishing, and farming.

The first European to visit Louisiana and Alabama was probably the Spaniard Álvar Nuñez Cabeza de Vaca, who traveled throughout the region by land in 1528. His countryman Hernando de Soto visited Alabama, Mississippi, and Louisiana between 1539 and 1542. Despite these early explorations and the nearby presence of a Spanish colony in Florida, the Spanish did not settle this part of the South. Instead, the French set about creating a colony in what they called Louisiana almost 20 years after Frenchman Robert de La Salle's exploration of the Mississippi River in 1682.

The French had made one attempt already to establish a settlement in the region. Robert de La Salle, Pierre's old hero, had tried to found a Gulf Coast colony in 1684, two years after he navigated the great Mississippi River to its mouth. With a group of nearly 500 soldiers and settlers, he had sailed west across the Gulf of Mexico. But because of a navigational error, he missed the fan-shaped delta that marks the mouth of the Mississippi, and his party ended up coming ashore at Matagorda Bay in Texas. Over the next two years, La Salle undertook three unsuccessful missions to find the Mississippi River. Meanwhile, the little settlement struggled against intolerable heat, Indian attacks, disease, and hunger. La Salle finally set out on an overland trek to French settlements further north. On March 19, 1687, he was murdered somewhere in Texas by two of his men who were frustrated with their slow progress. The Matagorda Bay settlement was left to perish.

The men who murdered La Salle were themselves killed in retaliation by other members of the party. Only six men in the La Salle expedition survived and reached a French outpost on the Mississippi.

In 1698, France again planned to settle the region. With his military experience and travel in the New World, as well as his desire to aid French colonial ventures, Pierre le Moyne d'Iberville was a natural choice to lead the mission. Iberville was granted a charter from King Louis XIV in 1698 to build a colony at the mouth of the Mississippi. His orders were to find "the mouth [of the Mississippi], . . . select a good site which can be defended with few men, and . . . block entry to the river by other nations." Iberville chose his brother Jean Baptiste le Moyne de Bienville to accompany him. Several other le Moyne brothers would follow later.

On October 24, 1698, a fleet under Iberville's command set sail from Brest, a seaport on the north-west coast of France. Iberville had two 30-gun frigates, the *Badine* and the *Marin*, and two smaller ships, the *Precieux* and the *Biscayenne*. Several small traversiers for exploring coastlines and rivers were on board. The ships also carried about 200 soldiers and colonists, including women, children, and a priest from La Salle's expedition.

In Haiti, then called Saint-Domingue, the fleet was strengthened by the addition of a 52-gun war-ship, the *François*. Then the ships sailed along the coast of Florida, stopping briefly near the Spanish settlements at Apalachicola Bay and Pensacola Bay. On January 31, 1699, the five vessels in Iberville's fleet anchored just outside what is now known as Mobile Bay on the coast of Alabama. This large bay extends about 25 miles north from its entrance to a point where it is fed by the Mobile and Tensaw

Haiti is the western part of the island of Hispaniola, which was discovered by Columbus in 1492. Although the entire island was claimed by the Spanish, who named it Santo Domingo, by the seventeenth century France was using the western end as a base for piracy. After the French began to establish plantations, the Spanish turned over the western part of the island to them in 1697. France renamed the region Saint-Domingue.

Rivers. For several days, Iberville, Bienville, and the other settlers explored the bay, taking measurements of the depth in the hope the body of water could provide a safe anchorage for their ships. Bad weather forced them to curtail their exploring and take refuge on Dauphin Island, just west of the bay's mouth.

When the weather cleared, Iberville ordered the ships to sail again. The small fleet now traveled west along the coast of present-day Mississippi. Storm winds soon forced them to anchor once more, this time in a small bay behind the island now known as Ship Island, not far from the coast and modern-day Biloxi, Mississippi. About three quarters of the colonists disembarked at Ship Island, where they erected huts and began clearing land. Meanwhile, Iberville, Bienville, and several dozen others in the party explored the coastline. Traveling by canoe, they made their way up the Pascagoula River and made contact with members of the Muskogean-speaking Bayogoula and Mougoulacha tribes who were hunting in the region. From the Indians, Iberville learned he was within easy sailing distance of the Mississippi River.

On February 27, two traversiers were prepared to set sail along the Gulf Coast. Most of the crew members who were chosen for the Mississippi River expedition were either French Canadians with experience surviving in the wild or buccaneers enlisted in Saint-Domingue. Twenty men went with Iberville and Bienville in one of the boats. An equal number were in the second traversier under the command of Sauvole de la Villantray. Each of the vessels carried

Buccaneers were pirates. They got their name from the French word *boucanier*, which meant "to cure meat," because they smoked stolen meat over fires on the beaches.

"Leaving my ships, we set out on the 27th [of February] for Malbouchia—the name given by the savages on this coast to the Mississippi— with two long boats, some bark canoes, and fifty-three men. We entered the river on March 2d, 1699. I found it obstructed by mud banks and logs of wood, partially petrified."

—Iberville, describing the mouth of the Mississippi, 1699

Not knowing of La Salle's death, Henri de Tonti had set out in 1686 for the lower Mississippi in search of his former commander. When he failed to find La Salle, Tonti left a letter with an Indian chief near the mouth of the Mississippi, instructing him to give the letter to the first Frenchman he saw.

provisions for about 20 days as well as arms and ammunition.

Rain fell as Iberville and the others in his party left the safe anchorage behind Ship Island. For several days, the little boats were battered by northerly winds as they sailed in the shallows not far from shore. They made their way through a maze of small islands and twisted shoreline as Iberville kept watch for signs of an opening that might be the mouth of the river. Finally, on March 2, he spied the inlet we now know as North Pass, one of more than a half-dozen inlets to the Mississippi Delta carved by the great river in its rush to the sea.

Once the adventurers sailed into the mouth of the river, Iberville saw signs that it was indeed the Mississippi. The water was fresh and looked like watery milk, just as La Salle had described it. But to be sure he was actually on the great river, Iberville decided to continue north upstream in search of Indians who could provide him with proof.

Going against the current, Iberville, Bienville, and the others slowly made their way upriver. North of the present-day site of New Orleans, they reached the village of the Bayogoulas. Their chief showed them a European-made cloak, which he claimed Henri de Tonti, a French explorer, had given to him. Still, the men were not yet sure this really was the Mississippi.

In their travels up the river, Bienville was a particularly valuable member of the expedition party because he was able to pick up the native languages with incredible ease. His ability to communicate with the Indians they met helped them build trust and also obtain information. Soon the group found another clue to the river's identity. Iberville and Bienville learned that an Indian chief near the mouth of the river possessed a letter—called the "speaking bark" by the Indians—that Henri de Tonti had left with him 13 years earlier.

Turning south again in search of the letter, the explorers split into two groups, led by Iberville and Bienville. Iberville's party passed through Lake Pontchartrain, the huge lake that borders present-day New Orleans. Bienville, with the main body of explorers, retraced the path they had followed in their earlier ascent of the river. When he neared the river's mouth, Bienville sent out word to the tribes in the region that he would give a reward for the speaking bark left by the Frenchman. Soon, an Indian appeared in his camp with Tonti's letter. Because there was no doubt about the origin of the letter, the French finally knew that this river was, indeed, the Mississippi.

Marche du Calumet de Paix.

The French watch as Indians in a village along the Mississippi River perform the march of the peace pipe to symbolize peaceful relations.

The English colony of Carolina (spelled Carolana at first) technically stretched from sea to sea, bringing it into conflicting claims with Spanish Florida and French Louisiana, as indicated by the title of one explorer's book, *Description of the English Province of Carolana, by Spaniards called Florida, and by the French La Louisiane.*

Now Iberville could turn his attention to founding a settlement. After searching for a suitable spot, he determined to start his colony on the hot sandy banks of Biloxi Bay. There, on April 8, 1699, about 90 settlers and some of the soldiers began building a fort on a bluff overlooking the bay. The oak-log fort was armed with cannon, land was cleared, and peas and corn were planted. Livestock, including a few pigs, cows, and a bull, were brought ashore, along with a forge for making metal goods.

On May 3, 1699, Iberville departed for France to obtain supplies and recruit additional colonists. He left the fledgling settlement under the command of Sauvole de la Villantray with Bienville as his assistant. Following his brother's departure, Bienville, a young man of only 19, led expeditions exploring the lower reaches of the Mississippi. He also scared off an English ship on an expedition to explore the territory for Carolina.

But the Biloxi settlement was in trouble. The summer heat was terrible, the water almost undrinkable, and food scarce. Like the English at Jamestown almost a century earlier, many colonists wasted hours searching for gold instead of planting crops. The situation grew even worse when about 20 French Canadians made their way down to Mississippi to join the colony, bringing only their appetites.

Iberville finally returned to the Biloxi settlement on December 7, 1699, with about 60 new colonists and badly needed provisions. An illness—probably yellow fever—and hunger had already killed many of the settlers he'd left behind.

Not long after his return, Iberville decided to erect a fort on a bluff overlooking the river near present-day Phoenix, Louisiana. This outpost, designed to prevent any trespassing by the English, was completed in February 1700. Called Fort de la Boulaye, it was put under Bienville's command.

As this fort was under construction, Iberville and Bienville resumed their explorations, traveling north up the Mississippi to the Red River. Bienville continued upstream on the Red River to present-day Natchitoches, Louisiana. These explorations convinced Iberville that the Mississippi valley must be held by the French at all costs. In late May, only a few months after his arrival, he again left Sauvole and Bienville in charge and set sail for Paris. He hoped to persuade the French government to fund the colonization of the Mississippi River region.

For the next year, Iberville remained in Paris, pleading for support for the colony in Louisiana. Unfortunately, most French officials were more eager to battle the Spanish for their colonies than invest in founding a new one. While Iberville was away, the Biloxi settlement was again ravaged by yellow fever. Among those who died was Sauvole. Bienville, now in command, decided to move the settlements to what he thought would be a better site on the Mobile River in present-day Alabama, about 50 miles upstream from Mobile Bay. Fort St. Louis was erected to protect the new settlement.

Iberville returned to the colony in December 1701, but he only stayed a short time before sailing back to Paris to try once again to obtain help from

"Boulaye" apparently referred to a grove of birch trees that once grew on the site of the fortification. The settlement never amounted to more than a small fort and a few houses.

the French government. Unfortunately, France was almost destitute, and all its resources were diverted into war with England. Although Iberville planned to return to the Gulf Coast in 1703, his health was flagging, probably as the result of yellow fever. He never saw Louisiana again. Instead, Iberville died in Havana, Cuba, on July 9, 1706, while on a military expedition to drive the English from the West Indies.

In the years after his older brother's departure, Bienville remained in command of the colony. He sent out expeditions to explore the huge territory of French Louisiana, reaching what is now Arkansas and Tennessee, as well as learning more about Louisiana, Mississippi, and Alabama. To oppose English advances into the region, he created military alliances as well as trading agreements with the Alabama, Mobile, Choctaw, and Chickasaw Indians.

Despite these successes, life was hard in the French colony. Bienville had trouble encouraging agricultural development, and yellow fever continued to take its yearly tolls. Many colonists left to go upriver to more established French settlements such as Peoria in present-day Illinois. Iberville's death in 1706 also caused unrest in the colony, and Bienville had his share of enemies.

Part of the problem was that the French never settled down anywhere. The Fort St. Louis site was too marshy, and the settlement moved once again in 1710 to avoid flooding. This time they dug in at the present-day site of Mobile, Alabama.

Confident in the importance of the Mississippi River for the French fur trade, King Louis XIV decided in 1712 to find a company to develop Louisiana. Antoine Crozat was granted a trading monopoly and other rights in the territory. The following year, Crozat removed Bienville as governor and replaced him with Antoine de la Mothe Cadillac, who had earlier founded a French colony in Detroit, Michigan. From 1713 to 1716, Bienville served as Cadillac's second in command.

While the French established many trading posts along the Mississippi and other rivers during these years, inflation in Louisiana was so high that soldiers could not even afford to feed and clothe themselves on their pay. In addition, Cadillac quickly destroyed the good relations Bienville had maintained with the Native Americans. It was no surprise that the Natchez Indians rose against the settlers in 1716.

However much he disagreed with Cadillac's policies, Bienville was a loyal Frenchman. He put down the Natchez uprising and established a fort and trading post at a Natchez village north of modern-day New Orleans on the Mississippi River. Named Fort Rosalie, this post became the center of a significant settlement that later grew to become the town of Natchez, Mississippi.

In late 1716, Cadillac was recalled to France. Antoine Crozat gave up on the Mississippi settlement in 1717 and returned his patent to the French ruler. The king soon located other investors and turned the region over to a company founded by a financier named John Law. Once again, Bienville was made colonial governor of French Louisiana.

"He has put such consternation in this country that, from the highest to the lowest, all [settlers] are asking with insistence to go out of it."
—Bienville, complaining about Cadillac, 1713

Surveyors and laborers work to erect Fort Rosalie, beginning with a sturdy log palisade for defense.

Thanks to Bienville's hard work and Law's financial wheeling and dealing, colonists began flocking to the region as excited investors ponied up more and more cash to fund the colonization of French Louisiana by Law's Mississippi Company. In 1717, Bienville constructed a fort just north of today's Montgomery, Alabama, on the Alabama River. He also oversaw the building of a trading post at the present-day site of Natchitoches, Louisiana.

When Bienville and his older brother first explored the Mississippi River in 1699, he had spotted a site on the river's east bank about 80 miles from its mouth. The young explorer thought this location would be perfect for a capital city. Nearly two decades later, in 1718, Bienville finally set out to build this city. Workmen labored to clear land and lay out the city streets, and houses made from brick and fences of native cypress wood began to rise in the city Bienville named New Orleans.

The new city grew rapidly, mostly due to the promotions of John Law in France. To attract permanent settlers, Bienville arranged to have a shipload of unmarried women sent to the city from France. Chaperoned by Catholic nuns until suitable husbands were found, the women were courted by Louisiana's adventurers and trappers. Bienville also

Bienville's New Orleans— now the French Quarter of the city—was laid out along the Mississippi behind an embankment and trench that prevented flooding. There was a brickyard on the edge of town (at right) and a market along the embankment. Warehouses and offices were close to the river. A monastery is marked by a cross near the town's center.

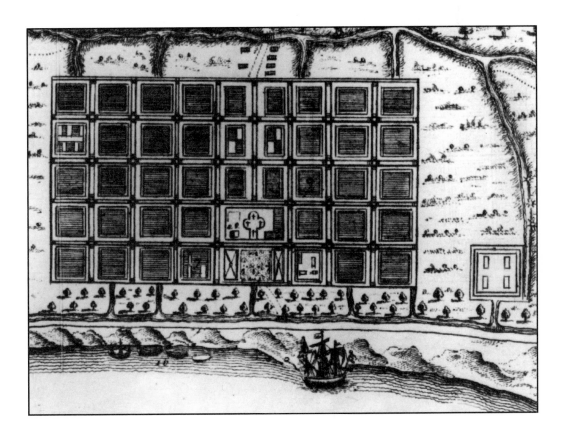

welcomed immigrants from all nations to the young settlement. By 1722, the city had become the capital of the territory.

Still, many of the new colonists died because they were not given the shelter and provisions pledged to them by promoters. These were not the only promises broken by John Law. In 1720, the so-called "Mississippi Bubble" burst when speculators

Crowds of people buying and selling shares of Mississippi Company stock. Many investors lost their life savings when the value plummeted.

discovered that Law's claims of riches to be found in French Louisiana were false. People from all over Europe lost money in the scheme, and Law had to flee France in disgrace. By the time the Mississippi Company stocks crashed, however, the influx of settlers John Law had started guaranteed the colony's success.

Financially ruined by the Mississippi Bubble and often blamed for Louisiana's failures, Bienville continued governing the colony until 1724. That year, legal problems forced him to return to France, where he was stripped of his office. Eight years later, in 1732, he again accepted the post as governor of Louisiana. He was greeted "with a joy and satisfaction without parallel" and served as governor for the next 10 years. This period was unfortunately marked by continuing conflicts with both the Natchez and the Chickasaw Indians.

Finally, after years of facing the difficulties of governing a colony, Bienville begged to be allowed to retire. He got his wish. On May 10, 1743, Bienville returned to France. Sadly, he lived long enough to see France sign over much of the colony to Spain in 1762. At the time of Jean Baptiste le Moyne de Bienville's death at the age of 88 in 1768, England and Spain were wrestling for control of the former French colony. Despite complaints of the French colonists who did not want to live under either English or Spanish rule, France was no longer involved in the settlement of the territory.

French Louisiana after Iberville and Bienville

As in other frontier territories, when the European population increased, Native Americans living in this southern region were pushed off their lands. While the Choctaws retreated, the Chickasaws and the Natchez fought back. But they were ultimately no match for the white settlers.

In 1762, following the French and Indian War, the land that now comprises the state of Louisiana was ceded to Spain. The region that includes much of western Florida, Alabama, and Mississippi was turned over to the control of the British a year later.

Although the Spanish had hoped to colonize what had been French territory in Louisiana, their plans were thwarted. Despite the fact that the region was in Spanish hands, the French population continued to increase as French settlers, driven from Nova Scotia in Canada by the British, began migrating in large numbers. In 1800, the Spanish government gave up any attempt to colonize the region and returned it to the French. Three years later, in 1803, the land west of the Mississippi was sold to the United States as part of the Louisiana Purchase. Louisiana was established in 1812, joining the union as the eighteenth state.

The Gulf Coast region between the Mississippi River and what is now the western boundary of Florida, meanwhile, fell into Spanish hands in 1779. It remained a Spanish territory until 1795, when the newly independent United States took control. In 1798, the Mississippi Territory—comprising modern-day Mississippi and parts of Alabama—was formed and, in 1817, Mississippi became the 20th state to join the Union. Two years later, Alabama became the 22nd state.

By the early 1800s, most Indian tribes who had lived along the Gulf Coast had been destroyed or driven out by wars with Americans. Many were transported to reservations in what is now Oklahoma.

Louisiana, Mississippi, and Alabama were slave states with plantations growing cotton, and, in Louisiana, also sugar cane. The states were quick to secede from the Union after Abraham Lincoln was elected president in 1860. The Confederate president, Jefferson Davis, was a Mississippian.

Bienville's great city of New Orleans thrives nearly three centuries later. Named for Philip II, duke of Orleans, who ruled France while King Louis XV was still a child, the city keeps its French heritage alive in Creole food, the Creole language (a hybrid of French and English), and zydeco music, which blends French lyrics and melodies with the musical rhythms of the Blues.

Soldiers fire a salute to the U.S. flag raised over New Orleans after the 1803 Louisiana Purchase.

140

Chapter Seven

James Oglethorpe
and the
Founding of Georgia

An accomplished politician and brilliant thinker, few people of his time would have seemed more qualified than James Oglethorpe to plan a colony in the New World. "He founded GEORGIA, gave it laws and trade," pointed out a rhymester upon his death. But, the satirical poet added, "He saw it flourish, and he saw it fade!" However promising Oglethorpe's dream seemed, the reality of colonization in Georgia, as in other colonies, was often far different than expected.

James Oglethorpe was born in London on December 22, 1696. He was the ninth and last child of Sir Theophilus and Lady Eleanor Oglethorpe. His father was a soldier and political leader, and his Irish mother had long been in service to the royal family.

This painting of General James Oglethorpe (1696-1785), hangs at Oglethorpe University in Atlanta, Georgia. It is considered the only true portrait of the general.

King William III (1650-1702) was the first cousin of his wife, Queen Mary II. Their grandfather was King Charles I, and Mary was the daughter of King James II.

At the time of Oglethorpe's birth, England was in political turmoil. The nation was split into two camps. On one side of the schism were the so-called Jacobites, followers of Catholic king James II, who had been forced to give up the throne and flee to France in 1688. On the other side were loyalist followers of King William III and Queen Mary II, Protestants who ruled after King James left England.

Although Theophilus was a Protestant, both he and Lady Eleanor, who was Catholic, were ardent Jacobites because of their long association with King James. They spied for him and led plots to return him to power. Because of their efforts, the family had to leave England for the safety of the exiled king's court in France. But ultimately, religion was more important to Theophilus Oglethorpe than his political loyalty. When King James demanded that he convert to Catholicism, Theophilus returned to England and pledged loyalty to King William III in autumn 1696. (Queen Mary II had died in 1694.) Jamie, as James Oglethorpe was called by his family, was born in the midst of this turmoil. Despite his Jacobite history, Theophilus served as a member of Parliament in the next few years.

Jamie was only five years old when his father died in 1702. Lady Eleanor quickly whisked the family back to France, her devotion to King James steadfast. Jamie's childhood must have been chaotic with all the family moves and Jacobite plots. Still, he managed to get an excellent education. He attended Eton, the famous preparatory school, and then became a student at Oxford University in 1714.

But Jamie thirsted for travel and adventure. He also was developing the Jacobite passions of his mother. After just two years at Oxford, he left for France, where his mother and three of his sisters were at the court of James III near Paris. (James III was the son of James II, who died in 1701). Jamie joined the army and battled the Turks. The brave young man was almost killed in combat he described as "very bloody and sharp."

When the fighting ended in late 1717, James Oglethorpe returned to the Jacobite court in Paris. As one of his brothers praised him, "he is entirely affectionate to the King." By 1719, however, it was clear that the Jacobite cause was lost. Oglethorpe went back that year to the family lands in England.

Oglethorpe was not any more handicapped by his Jacobite past than his father had been. Somehow, he also managed to avoid consequences for what we would consider to be serious offenses. In early 1722, he won a seat in Parliament despite having stabbed a man from an opposing political party. After his election, Oglethorpe killed a man in a brothel, but he escaped prosecution.

Oglethorpe may have been overzealous in defending himself from insult in his youth. As he matured, however, he became enraged about injustices faced by others. In 1728, he wrote a pamphlet called "The Sailor's Advocate." This tract detailed the horrible treatment of English sailors and argued that the practice of impressment, in which poor men were seized and forced to become sailors in the English navy, was illegal and morally wrong. His

Eton, properly called Eton College, is one of the world's most famous schools. Founded in 1440 by King Henry VI, the school was more than 250 years old when Oglethorpe enrolled as a student. To this day, students still sing in chapel, "King Henry, be a friend to us in trouble, that by your prayers we may be saved from eternal death."

pamphlet did little to improve the lot of the common seaman, but it marked the emergence of Oglethorpe as a humanitarian activist. His energy and commitment would save countless lives.

In late 1728 or early 1729, Oglethorpe learned that a friend named Robert Castell had been imprisoned as a debtor. Unable to bribe his jailers to put him in a better cell, Castell was locked up with small-pox victims. Within days, he was dead.

It was common for debtors in those days to be thrown in prison simply because they could not pay their bills. There they would rot in dirty and over-crowded cells until some friend or family member was able to buy their freedom. Stories like Castell's were not unusual. Had it not been for Oglethorpe, who immediately began speaking out in favor of prison reform, his death might have gone unnoticed. In February 1729, Oglethorpe was named chairman of a parliamentary inquiry into prison conditions.

Oglethorpe was sickened by what he saw as the committee toured England's prisons. In his report to Parliament, he described scenes of torture and shocking sanitary conditions. The poorest prisoners, who had nothing to give the jailers, were tied to dead bodies and left to suffer for weeks on end. Due to Oglethorpe's work, the penal system was overhauled, and several hundred debtors were freed.

Once released, however, these men and women were immediately back on the streets of London, out of work and hungry. Oglethorpe described the "miserable wretches . . . starving about the town for want of employment." But he had an idea. Soon

The parliamentary committee headed by Oglethorpe found Thomas Bambridge, the chief jailer at one of London's jails, guilty "of great extortions, and the highest crimes and misdemeanors in the execution of his . . . office." Bambridge had, the committee reported, "arbitrarily and unlawfully loaded with irons, put into dungeons, and destroyed prisoners for debt, under his charge, treating them in the most barbarous and cruel manner."

after the prison investigation ended, Oglethorpe proposed founding a colony in North America where England's unemployed could have a chance to make a living by working the abundant land. With unflagging zeal, he began seeking the money he needed to make his proposal a reality.

At that time, England's colonies stretched along the eastern seaboard from Maine to South Carolina. South Carolina's southern border was open to attack by Indians, the French, and the Spanish in Florida. Because the English government needed a defensive buffer between South Carolina and Florida, Oglethorpe would get his wish for a philanthropic colony.

Soon, Oglethorpe found 19 other people who shared his vision. Like him, they were wealthy men with charitable hearts, and many had served with Oglethorpe on the prison inquiry committee. In 1730, this group asked King George II for a charter to found a colony in America. Two years later, on June 20, 1732, the charter was finally granted.

Georgia stretched from sea to sea because people still believed the continent was quite slim. For practical purposes, though, the colony's northern boundary was the Savannah River, and the Altamaha River marked the southern border (now roughly the northern half of Georgia). Oglethorpe and his associates, named trustees of the colony, would run Georgia for 21 years, and then the king would take control. To prevent them from abusing their positions for personal gain, trustees could not own land, hold office, or profit from their work in the colony.

"Many of our poor subjects, if they had means to defray their charges of passage, . . . would be glad to settle in any of our provinces in America where by cultivating the lands, at present waste and desolate, they might . . . gain a comfortable subsistence for themselves and families."
—James Oglethorpe

King George II (1683-1760), shown here, and his father, George I, were actually German. George I became king of England because his mother was the grand-daughter of King James I.

Georgia before Oglethorpe

Spain reached Georgia in the early years of exploration, with Lucas Vazques de Ayllón landing on the Sea Islands off the Georgia coast in 1521. When Hernando de Soto first explored Georgia in about 1540, he found Choctaw, Cherokee, and Creek Indians, descendants of the Mound Builders who were the earliest known inhabitants of the region. The Cherokees, the largest of the tribes in the area, spoke an Iroquois dialect, while the Creek spoke a Muskogean language.

Spanish Florida extended into present-day Georgia in the 1560s. The Spaniards established trading relations with the Indians, most notably a chief named Guale. The Spanish set up missions and forts in the area Florida governor Pedro Menéndez de Avilés called Guale in the chief's honor.

The English, however, considered the region to be theirs. After a century of conflict with the English and later with the French and Indians, Spain finally abandoned most of its century-old missions in Guale in 1686. But the land continued to be a battleground for the next 50 years as Indian alliances changed and English, French, and Spanish settlers all tried to maintain their claims to Georgia and the surrounding territories.

The trustees would provide all necessities for settlers, including a cooking pot, a frying pan, three wooden bowls, and a Bible for every family.

The Georgia trustees went to work immediately. Oglethorpe's friend, John Percival, was named president of the colony while Oglethorpe was put in charge of fundraising and publicity. Oglethorpe's efforts were so successful that people all around England made contributions. A pamphlet he wrote described a pleasant "land of liberty and plenty" where settlers would immediately become landowners. "They are unfortunate, indeed," he promised, "if here they cannot forget their sorrows."

At first, James Oglethorpe did not plan to go to Georgia himself. But after his mother died in June 1732, he no longer felt the need to stay in England.

146

He and about 120 colonists sailed on the *Anne* on November 17 of that year. The settlers were mostly unemployed but respectable men and women and their families. A chaplain, a surgeon, an apothecary (pharmacist), and a civil engineer also went with the group. "As for provision," Percival reported, "medicines, tents, arms, etc., nothing is wanting."

The winter voyage across the Atlantic Ocean was difficult. Many passengers became seasick, and, as on all ocean voyages in those days, food and water were in short supply. The passengers—except for the officers and gentlemen like Oglethorpe—slept in narrow, coffin-like wooden berths four inches shy of six feet. Two infant boys who, Oglethorpe remembered, "were very weakly . . . and had indeed been half starved through want before they left London" died at sea. While this was sad, the passengers considered themselves fortunate to have lost only two people. Oglethorpe became godfather to a child born at sea, an infant named Georgius Warren.

On January 13, 1733, the *Anne* landed on the coast of South Carolina near Charles Town (today known as Charleston). After Oglethorpe went ashore to meet with the South Carolina governor, the settlers continued south and disembarked near Beaufort. As they were welcomed by the Carolinians there, Oglethorpe traveled south to the Savannah River. There he found the perfect spot for a settlement. The flat plain he chose, he wrote to the trustees, was "a healthy Situation . . . about Ten Miles from the Sea." The site of the future city was atop a bluff where the river curved like a half moon.

With his vast knowledge about colonizing North America and his connections with powerful officials in the government, John Percival, earl of Egmont, helped to make Oglethorpe's dream a reality.

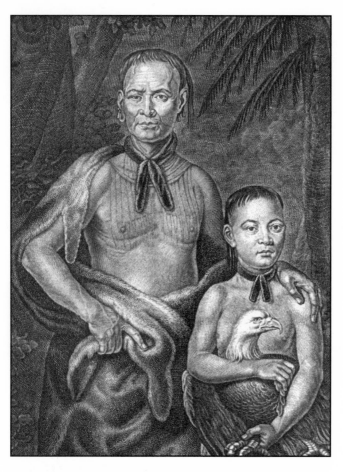

After returning to Beaufort, Oglethorpe led the other settlers and about 700 soldiers to the site. The group landed on February 12 and immediately began building the town of Savannah.

With the help of Mary Musgrove, the half-Indian wife of a trader, Oglethorpe and Chief Tomochichi soon met. Tomochichi was a Yamacraw, a member of the wide-ranging Creek Indian confederation. In May, the Creeks sent representatives to negotiate peace, trading pacts, and land grants. The Yamacraws and the rest of the Creeks ceded the land that was to be Georgia to

From 1733 until his death in 1739, Tomochichi was a personal friend of Oglethorpe as well as an ally. Oglethorpe granted the chief's wish that "his body might be buried amongst the English in the town of Savannah," and he served as a pallbearer at Tomochichi's funeral.

the settlers and signed a peace treaty and a trading agreement. The tribes also pledged to have no further dealings with the Spanish or the French. Treaties with the more distant Choctaws followed little more than a year later.

Savannah took shape quickly. Fortifications were built and houses raised. Like Philadelphia to the north, Savannah was laid out in squares with ample space reserved for parks. Each settler was given a lot in town for a home, along with a 5-acre

garden plot on the edge of town and a 45-acre farm in the country. Within a year, more settlers arrived. Savannah soon had a population of 400 people and about 40 completed homes.

The first summer in the new settlement was difficult. About 35 settlers died, including Georgia Close, the first baby born in the new colony. They fell ill and perished from the terrible heat and what was known as the "bloody flux" (dysentery).

By the summer of 1734, Oglethorpe had overseen the founding not only of Savannah, but also of some dozen other small communities. Like Rhode Island, Pennsylvania, and Maryland, Georgia was becoming a religious haven. The first Jews arrived in

At the 1733 treaty meeting, Tomochichi declared in gratitude to Oglethorpe and the English, "You confirmed our land to us, gave us food, and instructed our children: . . . The chief men of all our nation are here, to thank you for us; and before them, I declare your goodness; and that here I design to die; for we all love your people so well, that with them we will live and die."

Savannah's wooden houses, including Oglethorpe's, were about 24 feet long, 16 feet wide, and 8 feet high, not counting a small sleeping loft on the second floor. Every able-bodied man was granted 50 acres of land for himself and 50 for each servant he brought, but his total landholding could not exceed 500 acres. If a settler died without a male heir, his land reverted to the trustees according to what was known as the "tail-male" rule. Landholders were also forbidden to sell their land.

July 1733, and a group of Lutherans from Salzburg in what is now Austria made their way to the colony in the summer of 1734. Both groups thrived, as would the Scottish Presbyterians and Moravians (another Christian sect) who came soon after them.

As settlers arrived, the relationship between the colony and the trustees in England became strained. Oglethorpe was constantly seeking money, and the trustees suspected he was spending recklessly. They wanted a full accounting of activities in Georgia, so, in March 1734, Oglethorpe departed for England to report to the trustees.

Oglethorpe brought with him Tomochichi, Tomochichi's wife, and their grandnephew, as well as five Yamacraw warriors. Oglethorpe knew that the Yamacraws would be Georgia's best advertisement. The party was greeted with great fanfare. For the next year and a half, the Indians were entertained not only by the trustees but also by the king and queen.

Meanwhile, Oglethorpe mended fences with the trustees. On his advice, the trustees passed laws banning slavery, prohibiting the sale of rum, and regulating trade with the Indians. Oglethorpe was so convincing in his vision of Georgia's success that Parliament for the first time in history appropriated money for a colony. Early in 1736, Oglethorpe returned to Georgia with 300 new settlers.

For the next several years, Oglethorpe's time was devoted almost entirely to the colony's defense. He wanted to extend Georgia's border further south, but the Spanish still claimed the entire Georgia coast as their territory. Oglethorpe oversaw the construction of Fort Frederica on St. Simons Island to guard what was then the southern border of Georgia; Fort Augusta, about 150 miles up the Savannah River; and several smaller forts. In early 1737, he went back to England to raise more funds and recruit more soldiers. Oglethorpe became commander-in-chief of all the forces in South Carolina and Georgia. After returning to Georgia in September 1738, General Oglethorpe spent almost all his time with his frontier regiment at Fort Frederica.

The general's abilities as a military commander were soon tested. In 1739, war between Spain and England broke out in Europe and spread to America. During the next four years, Oglethorpe mounted

In early 1736, when Oglethorpe visited the Scottish settlement of Darien, south of Savannah on the coast, he wore a kilt in the Scottish style. Oglethorpe admired their village and the Scots, in turn, were faithful backers of Oglethorpe.

two attacks on the Spanish city of St. Augustine in Florida. Both of those maneuvers failed, but he was successful in protecting his colony against a 1742 invasion by Spaniards trying to defend their claim to the territory. Georgia would remain British.

During the years of fighting, Oglethorpe tried again and again to get financial help from Parliament and from South Carolina, which benefited from Georgia's defense. When no help came, Oglethorpe spent about 70,000 pounds of his own money—a fortune—to pay for the colony's militia and arms. The trustees not only refused financial assistance, but they also insulted Oglethorpe by appointing William Stephens as president of northern Georgia in 1741. Two years later, they gave Stephens the presidency of the whole colony.

Then, in 1743, Oglethorpe learned that a former officer in his colonial regiment was in London claiming that Oglethorpe had defrauded the trustees of money. In July 1743, Oglethorpe went back to London to defend himself. Confident that he would prevail, Oglethorpe also hoped to get compensation for the money he had spent on Georgia's military.

In 1744, a court-martial board found that the officer's charges against Oglethorpe were "either frivolous, vexatious or malicious." Oglethorpe also was repaid some of the huge amount of money that was owed to him. The experience, however, seemed to sour him on the idea of having anything more to do with Georgia. By 1749, Oglethorpe had stopped attending meetings of the trustees, and he never again returned to the colony he founded.

Resentful of the trustees' management of their lives, the settlers would not miss Oglethorpe. The general fought every one of the colonists' policy changes before his departure. In 1738, Georgians rejected the "tail-male" rule that had restricted land inheritance. The limitation on the amount of land a settler could own was removed in 1741. The next year, the prohibition against rum was abandoned.

Still, landholders eyed their neighbors in the Carolinas with envy. There, plantation slavery was enriching rice growers. Georgia planters finally shook free of the trustees' laws. After 1750, they could develop the plantation system they desired, for slavery had been made legal.

Because England depended on other countries to meet the high demand for silk, the trustees dreamed of guaranteeing Georgia's prosperity through manufacturing this fabric. Depending on the size of his landholding, every settler was required to plant at least 100 mulberry trees for silkworms. But silk was never produced successfully in Georgia because of the climate.

Slavery

African slavery was well established in the American colonies by the time Georgia's settlers won the "freedom" to have slaves in 1750. The first Africans had arrived in Jamestown, Virginia, in 1619 as servants. Historians still disagree about exactly when African slavery began in the American colonies, but the institution was definitely in place by the 1640s.

The first people to be enslaved were the native Indian populations in South and Central America, the Caribbean, and later in North America. These natives, however, were susceptible to European diseases. And since they were enslaved in their homelands, they often escaped or fought for their freedom. By the end of the 1600s, colonists increasingly turned to African slaves to solve their labor problems.

As the plantation system developed in the southern colonies, the demand for slaves to cultivate crops of tobacco, rice, and sugar cane increased. A trading network was set up to make slave trading even more profitable. Under this system, called the "triangular trade," ships left England and landed on the west coast of Africa, where goods were traded for captives.

After crossing the ocean, the ships docked at either the West Indies or the English colonies in North America, where slaves were traded for sugar or other products. The return voyage to England with a valuable cargo of colonial goods completed the triangle.

Cruelty to slaves reached new heights on the ships carrying blacks from Africa to the New World. These ships were jammed full of slaves, who were chained to keep them from revolting or jumping overboard.

Barely enough food, water, light, and ventilation were provided to keep the human cargo alive. Even then, about one of every five slaves died during the ocean voyage known as the "Middle Passage." Those who fell ill with smallpox or dysentery were simply thrown overboard.

It is estimated that between 8 to 15 million African slaves reached the Americas from the sixteenth through the nineteenth centuries, with as many as 6 million arriving during the eighteenth century alone.

This dramatic depiction of a slave market in West Africa shows slaves brought to the coast. Here they were inspected and marked before being detained to await their forced voyage to the New World. The Africans wearing hats and jewelry sold people from enemy tribes for textiles and other European goods.

Even with these changes to Georgia laws, many of the original settlers went to other colonies. A total of 5,500 colonists had come to Georgia, but only 3,000 remained in 1752. That year, the frustrated trustees gave the colony back to the Crown before the charter's term had even expired. Many viewed Georgia as a failure. Without interference from London, however, the colony gradually developed its plantation economy, growing rice and indigo and selling deerskins, lumber, beef, and pork.

Back in England, Oglethorpe took no part in Georgia's progress. In 1744, the 47-year-old had finally married. His wife was Elizabeth Wright, an heiress to a large fortune. But any hopes Oglethorpe had for enjoying a peaceful life were shattered the next year when Bonnie Prince Charlie, the son of James III, invaded Scotland and England in an attempt to seize the throne. The government called Oglethorpe to duty as a major general in command of a troop of cavalry. Before the general and his men saw any action, however, the Jacobite troops were on the run. Oglethorpe and his men gave chase, but they failed to stop the prince's escape. Suddenly, Oglethorpe's loyalty was questioned because of his former Jacobite leanings. In October 1746, he faced his second court-martial, this time on charges that he was derelict in his military duties. Although he was acquitted with honor and later promoted in rank to lieutenant-general, Oglethorpe never again saw active army service.

During all the years Oglethorpe had been in Georgia, he had retained his seat in the English

"The poor inhabitants of Georgia are scattered over the face of the earth; her plantations a wild; her towns a desert."
—a Georgia settler

Elizabeth Wright supported her husband with her inherited wealth during their long and happy marriage.

Parliament. He continued to hold this position until 1754, when he suffered an embarrassing defeat. For the remaining years of his life, General Oglethorpe focused his attention on the sciences and arts, becoming a member of a renowned literary circle that included the author Samuel Johnson and Johnson's biographer, James Boswell. He stayed healthy and strong until June 1785. But in the middle of that month, he fell ill. On June 30, General James Oglethorpe died at the age of 88.

Few people seemed to honor Oglethorpe's contributions after his death. Even James Boswell, who had praised him in 1783 as "the excellent and much honored General Oglethorpe," was silent about his passing until 1793, when he wrote "how sadly London was changed to me of late . . . [with] no General Oglethorpe." Oglethorpe might have wished to be remembered with the enthusiasm of one early visitor to Georgia. "He's extremely well beloved by all his People," wrote the observer. "The general Title they give him is FATHER. . . . His NAME justly deserves to be *Immortalized.*"

General James Oglethorpe at the sale of the books belonging to his deceased friend, Samuel Johnson, in February 1785. The artist marveled that the elderly Oglethorpe read this book without glasses.

Georgia from Colony to Statehood

After the trustees of Georgia turned over control of their colony to the British government in 1752, settlement continued and the economy of Georgia gradually grew stronger. Thanks to the plantation system and the use of slave labor, farmers and foresters had some success.

Most settlers in those years lived close to the Atlantic coast and on the Sea Islands. In about 1770, expansion to the interior of Georgia began in earnest. It would take almost 70 years before the region was completely settled by Americans, however, because the Creek and Cherokee Indians fiercely resisted giving up their lands. The sad conclusion of the Indians' struggle came in 1814 for the Creeks, with their defeat in the Creek War, and for the Cherokees in 1838. The Cherokees, who had steadily lost their holdings in northern

The U.S. Congress had passed an Indian Removal Bill in 1830, but the Cherokees fought the law successfully in the courts. Power remained on the side of the U.S. government, however, and the Cherokees were forced from their land.

Georgia, were forcibly removed in a march that came to be known as the "Trail of Tears" because about 4,000 of their people died on the 1,200-mile journey to present-day Oklahoma.

Georgia was deeply divided during the American Revolution, with about the same number of Loyalists as American patriots. In 1778, the port city of Savannah, founded by James Oglethorpe in 1733, was captured by British troops. Eventually, almost all of present-day Georgia was in British hands.

Once peace came, however, Georgia was ready to be a part of the new nation. In 1788, Georgia became the fourth state to join the Union.

Unheard-of prosperity arrived for Georgia planters after 1793, when a man named Eli Whitney invented the cotton gin to process cotton. Cotton then replaced rice and indigo, and Georgia, founded by paupers, became the wealthiest of the southern states because of the astounding success of what they called "King Cotton."

Because removing the seeds of cotton was very time-consuming, it was difficult to make money even when cotton prices were good. By mechanically separating the seeds from the fiber, the cotton gin made cotton production efficient and highly profitable.

A Southeastern Timeline

1492: Christopher Columbus lands in the West Indies and opens up New World exploration for the Spanish.

1498: Sailing for England, John Cabot is the first European to view Maryland.

1513: Spaniard Juan Ponce de León is the first European to explore Florida.

February 15, 1519: Pedro Menéndez de Avilés is born in Avilés, Spain.

1521: Ponce de León attempts to found a settlement in Florida.

1521: Spaniard Lucas Vazques de Ayllón lands on Georgia's Sea Islands.

1524: Italian Giovanni da Verrazano sails along the east coast of North America.

1526: Spanish sailors start a short-lived colony in North Carolina.

1528: Spaniard Álvar Nuñez Cabeza de Vaca visits Florida, Alabama, and Louisiana.

1539-1542: Hernando de Soto explores much of the Gulf Coast and the Southeast.

1552?: Sir Walter Raleigh is born in Devon, England.

1559: Tristán de Luna establishes a Spanish colony on Florida's Gulf Coast.

1562-1598: Persecuted Huguenots flee the Wars of Religion in France.

1562: French Huguenots under Jean Ribaut start a colony in South Carolina.

1564: French Huguenot René de Laudonnière builds Fort Caroline in northern Florida.

August 28, 1565: Pedro Menéndez reaches Florida.

September 1565: Menéndez founds Saint Augustine, Florida, the first permanent European settlement in North America.

September 20, 1565: Menéndez takes the French Fort Caroline.

Late September 1565: Menéndez executes hundreds of French Huguenots.

1566: Menéndez establishes missions in Guale, now the state of Georgia.

1566: Menéndez drives the French from present-day South Carolina and founds the town of Santa Elena.

1566: Pedro Menéndez Marqués explores the Chesapeake Bay for Spain.

1567: The French retake Fort Caroline.

1568: The Spanish are driven from the Florida Gulf Coast by the Calusa Indians.

September 17, 1574: Menéndez dies at the age of 55.

1576: The Spanish abandon their settlement at Santa Elena.

January 1580: John Smith is born near Willoughby in Lincolnshire, England.

1584: Sir Walter Raleigh receives a patent to colonize North America.

Summer 1584: The first **Raleigh** expedition explores the coast of what is now North Carolina and spots Roanoke Island.

Summer 1585: A second **Raleigh** mission goes to Roanoke under Richard Grenville.

1586: Englishman Sir Francis Drake destroys St. Augustine by fire.

June 1586: The Roanoke settlers under Grenville leave North Carolina after killing Roanoke chief Pemisapan.

July 1587: John White and the third **Raleigh** expedition land on Roanoke Island.

Early August 1587: English colonists massacre a group of Croatoan Indians.

August 18, 1587: Virginia Dare is the first English child born in North America.

Late August 1587: White leaves Roanoke to get aid from England. The settlers are never seen again.

1588: The Spanish Armada fleet attacks England; its defeat marks the beginning of English domination of the seas.

August 1590: White returns to Roanoke Island to find the settlement abandoned.

Early 1606: Cecil Calvert is born in the county of Kent, England.

April 1606: The Virginia Company is founded to promote colonization; it later becomes the Plymouth Company and the London Company.

1607: Leonard Calvert is born.

April 26, 1607: English colonists land on the Chesapeake Bay in Virginia.

Mid-May 1607: The English choose the site of Jamestown, Virginia.

June 1607: John Smith is allowed onto the council of Jamestown.

December 1607: Pocahontas saves **Smith** from execution by the Powhatan Indians.

Summer 1608: Smith explores and maps the Chesapeake Bay.

September 1608: Smith is elected president of Jamestown.

1609: Henry Hudson enters Delaware Bay.

Summer 1609: Lord De la Warr is appointed to replace **Smith** in Jamestown.

October 1609: Smith returns to England.

1612: Virginia colonist John Rolfe cultivates tobacco.

1614: Smith explores and maps New England.

1614: Pocahontas marries Rolfe.

October 29, 1618: Raleigh is executed at the age of about 66.

1619: The Virginia colony forms the house of burgesses, the first representative government in a North American colony.

1619: The first Africans are brought to Virginia as servants.

1622: Opechancanough's Powhatans kill one-third of Virginia's colonists.

1624: King James I revokes the Virginia Company's charter and makes Virginia a royal colony.

1629: King Charles I grants the Carolina territory to Robert Heath.

1631: The Dutch build a settlement at what is now Lewes, Delaware.

June 21, 1631: Smith dies at the age of 51.

1632: King Charles I grants what is now Maryland and Delaware to George Calvert.

April 15, 1632: Cecil Calvert inherits the land grant upon his father's death.

March 3, 1634: Leonard Calvert and the Maryland colonists land in their territory.

1638: Peter Minuit founds New Sweden on the site of today's Wilmington, Delaware.

1638: Leonard Calvert takes Kent Island in the Chesapeake Bay after several years of conflict with Virginia trader William Claiborne over rights to the land.

1638: Maryland passes its first body of laws, ending three years of standoffs between the assembly and the proprietors.

1642-1648: The English Civil War between the Puritans and the Cavaliers creates turmoil in the American colonies.

1645: Richard Ingle and Claiborne capture Maryland for the Puritans.

1646?: Henry Woodward is born, probably in Barbados.

1647: Leonard Calvert retakes Maryland.

June 9, 1647: Leonard Calvert dies at about the age of 40.

1649: Cecil Calvert enacts the Act of Toleration, guaranteeing religious freedom in Maryland.

1652: Puritans in Maryland overturn the Act of Toleration.

1655: The Dutch drive the Swedes from Delaware.

1655: Puritans seize the government in Maryland.

November 1657: Oliver Cromwell restores Maryland to **Cecil Calvert**.

July 1661: Pierre le Moyne d'Iberville is born in Montreal, Canada.

March 1663: King Charles II grants the Lords Proprietors a charter for Carolina.

May 29, 1664: Henry Woodward and 800 other English colonists land in what is now North Carolina.

1664: The British defeat of New Netherland makes Delaware English territory.

1666: Woodward and a party under Robert Sandford explore South Carolina.

1670: English colonists establish a settlement in South Carolina.

1670s: Explorers and fur traders venture into what is now West Virginia.

November 30, 1675: Cecil Calvert dies at the age of 69.

February 23, 1680: Jean Baptiste le Moyne de Bienville is born in Montreal, Canada.

1680: Charleston is founded in South Carolina.

1682: Woodward explores the interior of Carolina, opening trade routes.

1682: Pennsylvania acquires Delaware.

1682: Frenchman Robert de La Salle explores the Mississippi River from St. Louis to the Gulf of Mexico.

1684: La Salle accidentally lands in Texas when leading a mission to found a colony at the mouth of the Mississippi River.

1686: Woodward dies at about age 40.

1686: Frenchman Henri de Tonti, searching for La Salle, leaves a letter with Indians near the Mississippi Delta.

1686: Spain abandons most of its outposts in Georgia.

March 19, 1687: La Salle is murdered by his men while heading northeast for French settlements.

1688: The Calvert family loses control of Maryland to the monarchy.

1695: West African slaves cultivate rice in South Carolina.

December 22, 1696: James Oglethorpe is born in London.

1698: Iberville receives a charter from King Louis XIV to settle French Louisiana, the Gulf Coast area west of Florida.

March 2, 1699: Iberville and **Bienville** enter the mouth of the Mississippi River.

April 8, 1699: Iberville starts a colony on Biloxi Bay, Mississippi.

1699: Williamsburg replaces Jamestown as the capital of Virginia.

1701: Bienville builds Fort St. Louis on the Mobile River in Alabama.

1701: The people of Delaware agree to become part of Pennsylvania.

July 9, 1706: Iberville dies at the age of 45.

1710: Bienville founds a settlement at what is now Mobile, Alabama.

1712: North and South Carolina are made independent colonies.

1712: King Louis XIV grants Antoine Crozat a trading monopoly and the right to start settlements in the Mississippi valley.

1713: Antoine de la Mothe Cadillac replaces **Bienville** as governor of French Louisiana.

1715: Maryland is returned to the Calverts.

1716: Bienville puts down a Natchez Indian uprising in Mississippi and builds Fort Rosalie, now Natchez, Mississippi.

1716: Cadillac is recalled to France.

1717: Crozat gives up his right to settle the Mississippi valley territory.

1717: John Law starts the Mississippi Company to colonize French Louisiana.

1717: Bienville is again named governor of French Louisiana.

1718: Bienville builds New Orleans, Louisiana.

1720: Law's Mississippi Company collapses and investors lose all their money.

1724: Bienville loses his position because of the Mississippi Company scandal.

1729: King George II makes North and South Carolina royal colonies.

1730s: German and Scotch-Irish colonists begin to move south from Pennsylvania into western Virginia.

1732: Bienville once again becomes governor of Louisiana.

June 20, 1732: James Oglethorpe and the other trustees of Georgia receive a charter from King George II.

January 1733: Oglethorpe and the Georgia colonists land in North America.

February 12, 1733: Georgia colonists begin building Savannah.

May 1733: The Creek Indians sign a peace treaty and a trading agreement and cede land to the Georgia settlers.

March 1736: Oglethorpe begins constructing a fort on St. Simons Island, then near Georgia's southern border.

1741: William Stephens is named president of northern Georgia.

1742: Oglethorpe defeats the Spanish in Georgia, once part of Spanish Florida.

1743: Stephens becomes president of the entire Georgia colony.

1743: Bienville resigns as governor of Louisiana.

1744: Eliza Lucas Pinckney perfects the cultivation and processing of indigo in South Carolina.

1749: The Ohio Company is granted land by the British government, including what is now West Virginia.

1752: The trustees of Georgia turn over their colony to King George II.

1754-1763: The French and Indian War rages over control of inland territory until the French are defeated by the British.

1762: France gives Louisiana to Spain.

1763: England gains Mississippi, Alabama, and western Florida after winning the French and Indian War.

1763: England wins the rest of Florida from Spain after the Seven Years' War.

1768: Bienville dies at the age of 88.

1775-1783: The American colonies fight for independence from England in the Revolutionary War.

1779: Spain gains control of Mississippi and Alabama.

1783: Florida is returned to Spain at the end of the American Revolution.

June 30, 1785: Oglethorpe dies at the age of 88.

December 7, 1787: Delaware is the first former colony to join the United States. Dover has been its capital since 1777.

January 2, 1788: Georgia is the fourth state to join the U.S. Atlanta has been its capital since 1877.

April 28, 1788: Maryland becomes the seventh state to join the U.S., with its capital at Annapolis.

May 23, 1788: South Carolina joins the Union as the eighth state. Columbia has been its capital since 1786.

November 21, 1789: North Carolina becomes the twelfth state. Its capital has been at Raleigh since 1788.

1791: Maryland donates land to create the District of Columbia.

1793: Eli Whitney invents the cotton gin, transforming the southern economy.

1795: The U.S. retakes territory from Spain, including Mississippi and Alabama.

1798: The Mississippi Territory, including Mississippi and Alabama, is formed.

1800: Spain returns Louisiana to France.

1803: The U.S. buys the Louisiana territory from France, doubling its land mass.

April 30, 1812: Louisiana is the Union's eighteenth state, with Baton Rouge as its capital.

December 10, 1817: Mississippi enters the U.S. as the 20th state. Its capital has been at Jackson since 1821.

1819: Spain gives Florida to the U.S.

December 14, 1819: Alabama is the 22nd state to join the Union, with its capital at Montgomery.

1822: Florida is organized as a U.S. territory.

1830: The U.S. Congress passes the Indian Removal Bill, authorizing states to take Indians' land.

1842: In the Seminole War, Florida's Seminole Indians are defeated by the U.S.

March 3, 1845: Florida joins the U.S. as the 27th state. Its capital has been at Tallahassee since 1824.

June 20, 1863: West Virginia becomes the 35th state after separating from Virginia, with its capital at Charleston.

Source Notes

Quoted passages are noted by page and order of citation. Spelling and some capitalizations are modernized.

Chapter One

p. 13 (margin): Eugene Lyon, ed., *Pedro Menéndez de Avilés*, vol. 24 of *Spanish Borderlands Sourcebooks* (New York: Garland, 1995), xxiv.

p. 13 (all): Gonzalo Solís de Merás, *Pedro Menéndez de Avilés, Memorial*, trans. Jeannette Thurber Connor (Gainesville: University of Florida Press, 1964), 255.

p. 16: Solís de Merás, *Menéndez*, 261.

p. 20 (margin): Charles Bennett, ed., *Laudonnière and Fort Caroline: History and Documents* Gainesville: University of Florida Press, 1964, 142-143.

p. 22: Bartolome Barrientos, *Pedro Menéndez de Avilés, Founder of Florida*, trans. Anthony Kerrigan (Gainesville: University of Florida Press, 1965), 47.

p. 23 (caption): Solís de Merás, *Menéndez*, 87.

p. 26: Lyon, *Menéndez*, xx.

p. 28 (margin): William Dewhurst, *The History of St. Augustine, Florida* (1885; reprint, Rutland, Vt.: Academy, 1968), 64.

p. 31 (first): Solís de Merás, *Menéndez*, 256.

p. 31 (second): Solís de Meras, *Menéndez*, 37.

Chapter Two

p. 36 (margin): Robert Gray, *A History of London* (New York: Taplinger, 1979), 139.

p. 38: Margaret Irwin, *That Great Lucifer: A Portrait of Sir Walter Ralegh* (London: Chatto & Windus, 1960), 18.

p. 41: Karen Ordahl Kupperman, *Roanoke: The Abandoned Colony* (Totowa, N.J.: Rowman & Allanheld, 1984), 17.

p. 47 (margin): David Stick, *Roanoke Island: The Beginnings of English America* (Chapel Hill: University of North Carolina Press, 1983), 101.

p. 53 (margin): Kupperman, *Roanoke*, 157.

Chapter Three

p. 55 (caption): Bradford Smith, *Captain John Smith: His Life and Legend* (Philadelphia: J. B. Lippincott, 1953), 194.

p. 57 (margin): Smith, *Captain John Smith*, 28.

p. 58 (margin): Smith, *Captain John Smith*, 36.

p. 60: Smith, *Captain John Smith*, 71.

p. 62 (margin): Smith, *Captain John Smith*, 93.

p. 62: Smith, *Captain John Smith*, 93.

p. 64: Smith, *Captain John Smith*, 101.

p. 65 (margin): Lyon Gardiner Tyler, ed., *Narratives of Early Virginia, 1606-1625* (1907; reprint, New York: Barnes & Noble, 1952), 21.

p. 66 (caption): Smith, *Captain John Smith*, 147.

p. 66: Smith, *Captain John Smith*, 104.

p. 67 (caption): Tyler, *Narratives*, 326.

p. 68: Tyler, *Narratives*, 326.

p. 72: Smith, *Captain John Smith*, 181.

p. 76 (first): Smith, *Captain John Smith*, 247.

p. 76 (second): Smith, *Captain John Smith*, 252.

Chapter Four

p. 81 (margin): Ted Morgan, *Wilderness at Dawn: The Settling of the North American Continent* (New York: Simon & Schuster, 1993), 238.

p. 81: David Hawke, *The Colonial Experience* (New York: Macmillan, 1966), 109.

p. 85 (margin): Clayton Colman Hall, ed., *Narratives of Early Maryland, 1633-1684* (1910; reprint, New York: Barnes & Noble, 1953), 7-9.

p. 86 (first margin): Hall, *Narratives*, 16.

p. 86 (second margin): Hall, *Narratives*, 39-40.

p. 88 (margin): Hall, *Narratives*, 43-44.

p. 88: Hall, *Narratives*, 42.

Chapter Five

p. 103: Alexander S. Salley Jr., ed., *Narratives of Early Carolina, 1650-1708* (1911; reprint, New York: Barnes & Noble, 1953), 67.

p. 105: Salley, *Narratives*, 66.

p. 107 (first): Salley, *Narratives*, 91.

p. 107 (second): Salley, *Narratives*, 104.

p. 108 (margin): Salley, *Narratives*, 103-104.

p. 108: Salley, *Narratives*, 105.

p. 109 (margin): W. P. Cumming et al., eds., *The Exploration of North America, 1630-1776* (New York: Putnam, 1974), 91.

p. 110 (margin): Cumming, *Exploration*, 92.

p. 113: Cumming, *Exploration*, 92.

Chapter Six

p. 126: David Hayne, ed., *Dictionary of Canadian Biography*, vol.V (Toronto: University of Toronto Press, 1969), 456.

p. 128 (margin): J. F. H. Claiborne, *Mississippi as a Province, Territory and State*, vol. 1 (1879; reprint, Spartanburg, S.C.: The Reprint Co., 1978), 18.

p. 130 (margin): Claiborne, *Mississippi as a Province*, 19.

p. 133 (margin): Grace King, *Jean Baptiste le Moyne, Sieur de Bienville* (New York: Dodd, Mead, 1893), 198.

p. 137: Dumas Malone, ed., *Dictionary of American Biography*, vol. V (New York: Scribner's, 1939), 252.

Chapter Seven

p. 141: Phinizy Spalding, *Oglethorpe in America* (Chicago: University of Chicago Press, 1977), 2.

p. 143 (margin): John Morrill, ed., *The Oxford Illustrated History of Tudor and Stuart Britain* (Oxford: Oxford University Press, 1996), 259.

p. 143 (first): Amos Aschbach Ettinger, *James Edward Oglethorpe: Imperial Idealist* (Oxford: Clarendon Press, 1936), 68.

p. 143 (second): Ettinger, *James Edward Oglethorpe*, 74.

p. 144 (margin): Roy Porter, *London: A Social History* (London: Hamish Hamilton, 1994), 155.

p. 144: Ettinger, *James Edward Oglethorpe*, 110.

p. 145 (margin): Ettinger, *James Edward Oglethorpe*, 118.

p. 146 (both): Ettinger, *James Edward Oglethorpe*, 122.

p. 147 (first): Ettinger, *James Edward Oglethorpe*, 129-130.

p. 147 (second): Sarah Temple and Kenneth Coleman, *Georgia Journeys, 1732-1754* (Athens: University of Georgia Press, 1961), 6.

p. 147 (third): Ettinger, *James Edward Oglethorpe*, 132.

p. 148 (caption): Kenneth Coleman, ed., *A History of Georgia* (Athens: University of Georgia Press, 1977), 30.

p. 149 (caption): Spalding, *Oglethorpe in America*, 78-79.

p. 152: Ettinger, *James Edward Oglethorpe*, 253.

p. 155 (margin): Daniel J. Boorstin, *The Americans: The Colonial Experience* (New York: Random House, 1958), 95.

p. 156 (first and second): Ettinger, *James Edward Oglethorpe*, 327.

p. 156 (third): Ettinger, *James Edward Oglethorpe*, 141.

Bibliography

Andrews, Charles M. *The Colonial Period of American History*. Vol. 1. New Haven, Conn.: Yale University Press, 1964.

Barnwell, J. W. "Dr. Henry Woodward: The First English Settler in South Carolina and Some of His Descendants." *South Carolina Historical and Genealogical Magazine*, January 1907.

Barrientos, Bartolome. *Pedro Menéndez de Avilés, Founder of Florida*. Trans. Anthony Kerrigan. Gainesville: University of Florida Press, 1965.

Bennett, Charles, ed. *Laudonnière and Fort Caroline: History and Documents*. Gainesville: University of Florida Press, 1964.

Boorstin, Daniel J. *The Americans: The Colonial Experience*. New York: Random House, 1958.

Brandon, William. *Indians*. Boston: Houghton Mifflin, 1987.

Browne, William Hand. *George Calvert and Cecilius Calvert, Barons Baltimore*. New York: Dodd, Mead, 1890.

Burt, Jesse, and Robert B. Ferguson. *Indians of the Southeast: Then and Now*. Nashville: Abingdon Press, 1973.

Capps, Clifford, and Eugenia Burney. *Georgia*. New York: Thomas Nelson, 1972.

Claiborne, J. F. H. *Mississippi as a Province, Territory and State*. Vol. 1. 1879. Reprint, Spartanburg, S.C.: The Reprint Co., 1978.

Coleman, Kenneth, ed. *A History of Georgia*. Athens: University of Georgia Press, 1977.

Crouse, Nellis M. *Lemoyne d'Iberville: Soldier of New France*. Ithaca, N.Y.: Cornell University Press, 1954.

Cumming, W. P., et al., eds. *The Exploration of North America, 1630-1776*. New York: Putnam, 1974.

Deetz, James. *In Small Things Forgotten: An Archaeology of Early American Life*. New York: Anchor, 1996.

Dewhurst, William. *The History of St. Augustine, Florida*. 1885. Reprint, Rutland, Vt.: Academy, 1968.

Ettinger, Amos Aschbach. *James Edward Oglethorpe: Imperial Idealist*. Oxford: Clarendon Press, 1936.

Foster, James W. *George Calvert: The Early Years*. Baltimore: Museum and Library of Maryland History, Maryland Historical Society, 1983.

Gray, Robert. *A History of London*. New York: Taplinger, 1979.

Hall, Clayton Colman, ed. *Narratives of Early Maryland, 1633-1684*. 1910. Reprint, New York: Barnes & Noble, 1953.

Hawke, David. *The Colonial Experience*. New York: Macmillan, 1966.

———, ed. *U.S. Colonial History: Readings and Documents*. New York: Bobbs-Merrill, 1966.

Hodge, Frederick Webb, ed. *Handbook of American Indians North of Mexico*. 2 vols. Totowa, N.J.: Rowman and Littlefield, 1975.

Irwin, Margaret. *That Great Lucifer: A Portrait of Sir Walter Ralegh*. London: Chatto & Windus, 1960.

Kehoe, Alice Beck. *North American Indians: A Comprehensive Account*. Englewood Cliffs, N.J.: Prentice Hall, 1992.

King, Grace. *Jean Baptiste le Moyne, Sieur de Bienville*. New York: Dodd, Mead, 1893.

Kupperman, Karen Ordahl. *Roanoke: The Abandoned Colony*. Totowa, N.J.: Rowman & Allanheld, 1984.

Lemay, J. A. Leo. *The American Dream of Captain John Smith*. Charlottesville: University Press of Virginia, 1991.

Loewen, James W. *Lies My Teacher Told Me: Everything Your American History Textbook Got Wrong*. New York: Simon & Schuster, 1995.

Lyon, Eugene, ed. *Pedro Menéndez de Avilés*. Vol. 24 of *Spanish Borderlands Sourcebooks*. New York: Garland, 1995.

Morgan, Ted. *Wilderness at Dawn: The Settling of the North American Continent*. New York: Simon & Schuster, 1993.

Morrill, John, ed. *The Oxford Illustrated History of Tudor and Stuart Britain*. Oxford: Oxford University Press, 1996.

Ogg, Frederic Austin. *The Opening of the Mississippi: A Struggle for Supremacy in the American Interior*. 1904. Reprint, New York: Greenwood, 1969.

Porter, Roy. *London: A Social History*. London: Hamish Hamilton, 1994.

Robinson, W. Stitt. *The Southern Colonial Frontier, 1607-1763*. Albuquerque: University of New Mexico Press, 1979.

Salley, Alexander S., Jr., ed. *Narratives of Early Carolina, 1650-1708*. 1911. Reprint, New York: Barnes & Noble, 1953.

Smith, Bradford. *Captain John Smith: His Life and Legend*. Philadelphia: J. B. Lippincott, 1953.

Solís de Merás, Gonzalo. *Pedro Menéndez de Avilés, Memorial*. Trans. Jeannette Thurber Connor. Gainesville: University of Florida Press, 1964.

Spalding, Phinizy. *Oglethorpe in America*. Chicago: University of Chicago Press, 1977.

Stick, David. *Roanoke Island: The Beginnings of English America*. Chapel Hill: University of North Carolina Press, 1983.

Temple, Sarah, and Kenneth Coleman. *Georgia Journeys, 1732-1754*. Athens: University of Georgia Press, 1961.

Tyler, Lyon Gardiner, ed. *Narratives of Early Virginia, 1606-1625*. 1907. Reprint, New York: Barnes & Noble, 1952.

Ward, Harry M. *Colonial America, 1607-1763*. Englewood Cliffs, N.J.: Prentice Hall, 1991.

Wood, Peter H. *Black Majority: Negroes in Colonial South Carolina from 1670 through the Stono Rebellion*. New York: W. W. Norton, 1975.

Zinn, Howard. *A People's History of the United States*. New York: HarperCollins, 1990.

Index

About the Author

Kieran Doherty is a longtime journalist and business writer as well as a nonfiction writer for young adults. In addition to writing *Puritans, Pilgrims, and Merchants: Founders of the Northeastern Colonies*, he is the author of three other books in the **Shaping America** series: *Explorers, Missionaries, and Trappers: Trailblazers of the West*; *Ranchers, Homesteaders, and Traders: Frontiersmen of the South-Central States*; and *Voyageurs, Lumberjacks, and Farmers: Pioneers of the Midwest*. An avid sailor, he lives in Boynton Beach, Florida, with his wife, Lynne.

Photo Credits